easy **pewter** projects

dedication

This book is dedicated to everyone who has had problems with the budget on art and craft materials and then needed real creativity in trying to balance the books.

... and to

Helena Scheibe, who gave me my only two lessons in pewter shortly before she stopped teaching to nurse her ill husband. She shared her knowledge unselfishly with me, and so many people. Had it not been for her, I would never have found pewter. Helena, through her talent and passion, planted the seeds, then nurtured the roots and much of the tree, so the art of pewter could grow once again in South Africa. Many of us who enjoy pewter, whether we know it or not, are little fruits which grew from that tree.

Pewter Plus

Sandy Griffiths

David and Charles

A DAVID & CHARLES BOOK

David & Charles is an F+W Publications Inc. company

4700 East Galbraith Road

Cincinnati, OH 45236

First published in the UK in 2007

Originally published by Metz Press

1 Cameronians Avenue, Welgemoed, 7530 South Africa

Publisher   Wilsia Metz

Design and lay-out   Lindie Metz

Photographer   Ivan Naudé

Reproduction   Color/Fuzion

Copyright © Metz Press 2007

Text copyright © Sandy Griffiths

Photographs copyright © Metz Press

A catalogue record for this book is available from the British
Library.

ISBN-13: 978-0-7153-2797-5 paperback with flaps
ISBN-10: 0-7153-2797-6 paperback with flaps
Printed and bound in China by WKT Company for David
& Charles, Brunel House, Newton Abbot, Devon

Visit our website at www.davidandcharles.co.uk

Acknowledgements

Writing this book was a great journey. I met and spoke to people whom I never would have met or spoken to had I not had this opportunity. I enjoyed every little bit of banter and inspiration. So, of course, looking back, there are many people out there that I would like to thank, and mostly you don't know who you are.

There was the art-shop lady who photocopied the cover of a beautiful journal I could not afford to buy, so I could use the image for my scrapbooking project. There were my students who told me how marvellous I was and how they loved all my work – they gave me confidence. There were my students who saw my work and, significantly, said nothing – they inspired dry-mouthed fear and made me try harder. There were friends who offered to help out with designs. There were friends who offered their homes for the photoshoots. There was a friend who said "I saw so-and-so's book on such-and-such-a-craft – why don't you write a book on pewter? You can do a much better book than that!" so I was under pressure to prove her right. And one who said, "But you're not qualified to write a book? How are you going to do this?" with that "you really shouldn't be doing this" sound in her voice, so I was under pressure to prove her wrong. Those who said, " You're writing a book? Gosh, that's fantastic!" made me determined to have fun. There was a friend who said, "Don't just do a photocopied manual; do a book and get it published. I'll introduce you to a publisher" and did. There were friends who understood that I had been neglectful as I was neck deep in a project I really wanted to do. There was, of course, as there always is, the long-suffering family who had to pick up the pieces or simply walk over them and not moan because there wasn't anyone to listen. There were friends who said, "Don't worry, when your book is published we'll buy a copy, and we must go out and cel-ebrate". So please do, and yes, we definitely will.

So thank you, nkosi, dankie to all of you – those of you who know who you are and those of you who do not. I had lots and lots of fun writing this book.

Contents

Introduction

Pewter is a relatively soft metal that is easily moulded using simple techniques. Pewter work is a wonderful craft suitable for many personalities. All you really need to succeed at it is the will and the passion to learn and experiment with this metal that is so willing to be bent and moulded into all sorts of exciting shapes. Because it is so versatile, even repeating the same design seldom has exactly the same result. Pewter combines very well with other metals such as copper and can be embellished with paints and beads, allowing many decorative possibilities.

The next comforting thing about pewter work is that all designs are traced onto the metal. So if you feel you are held back by your inability to draw, fear not – simply find a design you like, size it on a photocopy machine and trace away (bearing in mind that you cannot copy designs if you do pewter work for commercial gain). Nearly all the designs used in this book have been included in the template section (see pages 119-128). And once you have finished your project it's complete. It doesn't have to be fired, heat set, sewn, sanded or vanished, which means you are less likely to land up with boxes filled with UFO's (un-finished objects).

There are two ways of working with pewter. First, relief modelling, which is the craft form explained in this book. This is worked on thin sheets of pewter. The design is traced onto the metal and then modelled from the back, using special tools, to create a raised or relief design on the front. The back is filled with beeswax to prevent the soft metal from being flattened. The front of the design is treated with a chemical substance called patina to give the metal an aged effect. The completed design is then secured onto a firm surface to support the pewter. Pewter relief-modelling is used for decorative purposes.

Working with cast pewter, on the other hand, is a completely different craft from what this book is all about, although the same metal is used. It requires special skills, and involves melting down the pewter and pouring it into moulds to make items such as wine goblets, bowls and serving spoons. The earliest known use of cast pewter was in China over 2 000 years ago.

Pewter relief-modelling is not a new craft – it has been done, on and off, for years. There is very little information readily available on the craft, but through speaking to many people I have learnt some interesting facts. It appears to have been popular around the late forties to around the late sixties, early seventies. Many older people tell me they did pewter at school. And I have seen some very beautiful items made by students' grandmothers and grandfathers. One of the popular items from that time is the pewter-framed mirror. The basic method as well as the materials and tools used have changed very little. Beeswax was used to support the high relief design as is the case today. The very early tools were made of blown glass. These have evolved to the tools we use today, which are metal with plastic or wooden handles. The shape of the tool, where it meets the pewter, has remained unchanged. In the early years paper pencils had not yet been invented, so the crafter would wrap a soft cloth or chamois over the tip of the tracer tool and use this instead.

I find it very exciting that we are practising this old craft in the same way it has always been done. When we sit down to do our pewter work, we are experiencing the same touch sensations and smells our grandparents did.

how to use this book

Read carefully through the book from the beginning. I have given lots of information about all the tools and materials needed. Start with the three beginner's projects which will take you through the two pewter techniques required, low relief and high relief. Please do not jump to the other projects before completing these. (I know it is tempting, the others look so much more exciting!) I take you through the basic steps slowly and discuss what to look out for with each step. I also explain why we need to follow each step, what it achieves and prevents. Keep in mind that I have designed these three projects specifically to introduce a novice to the techniques of pewter work.

Most importantly, have fun. Bear in mind that no two people will work exactly the same and no one person knows all there is to know. If you want to know if something can be done in pewter or with pewter – try it. Keep your small off-cuts of pewter for experimenting. That is how I learnt. Just keep experimenting.

Sandy Griffiths

sandy.craft@telkomsa.net

Materials & tools

Pewter work is often considered an expensive hobby. This is not so. It is no more expensive than hobbies such as fabric painting, decoupage, embroidery, mosaic, oil painting and so on. The unit price of sheet pewter is quoted per running metre, which makes it sound expensive. But there is probably no single project that will require a full metre. So don't be put off by the unit price. Consider the total cost of the project and you will be pleasantly surprised.

Pewter work requires a number of special materials, as well as dedicated tools which will be used over and over and will last many years. You don't need a large amount of storage or working space to enjoy this craft. The tools and materials you require will fit comfortably into a medium-sized box or tray (a cat-litter tray works well).

pewter sheets

These are thin sheets made up of lead, tin, and a little copper. The more tin in the make-up, the shinier the pewter will be. Most manufacturers place a thin layer of tin over the sheet to make it shinier. If you polish the pewter extensively, this layer of tin may be rubbed off and the layer underneath exposed. In some countries it is possible to obtain lead-free pewter. This is not widely available owing to cost.

Pewter has a right and a wrong side. The right side is not necessarily the shiny side. Compare the back with the front: the back has a bluish tint while the front is whiter. The non-technical way of telling is that all pewter comes in rolls, and the inside of the roll is the wrong side, while the outside of the roll is the right side. The patina does not work on the back, so if you are unsure, test on a small piece of pewter.

The pewter is very soft and may be easily cut with a pair of scissors or a craft knife (see cutting techniques on page 38). Because the pewter is a soft metal it must always be mounted onto something hard to give it support. Bottles, wooden boxes, frames, light-switch covers and tins are all suitable items to decorate with relief pewter-modelling. Pewter is sold by the metre in varying widths: either 30 cm or 48 cm.

work surface

You need a smooth, hard surface with no texture. A smooth wooden board or a piece of glass will do. Make sure you keep your work surface clean and free of scratches.

soft cloth

This is used when modelling the pewter. When you want the pewter to 'push out', you model on the soft cloth. If you try to model the

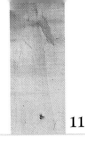

pewter on the hard surface it will remain flat, as it has nothing to mould into. Felt, yellow dusters, or a chamois is good to use.

How deep you are modelling the pewter will determine whether you will need a single, double or triple layer of cloth. Always add one extra layer at a time, as it is needed. If the layers of cloth are too thick, the pewter will buckle, as it will not have enough support.

lubricant

When working with tools on the pewter you will be working with metal on metal and therefore need a lubricant to help the tool move smoothly over the pewter. Without lubricant the tool will dig into the pewter. Use petroleum jelly, baby oil, cooking oil or liquid paraffin.

filler

This is used to fill in the back of a high-relief design to prevent the design from being pushed back or flattened. Beeswax works best as it hardens quickly, does not contract when cold, and sticks to the pewter. Do not use candle wax as this contracts when cold and crumbles easily. Heat the beeswax in an old jam tin. Use a glass dropper to drop beeswax into the back of the design. The wax should be completely liquid before using. If it starts solidifying in the dropper while it is being sucked it up, it needs to be hotter. The wax must be level with the pewter; any wax outside the design must be cleaned off with turpentine on cotton wool. Do not scratch it off with a tool or fingernail, as you will scratch into you design. Any beeswax left outside of the design will become a raised bump on the front once you start the polishing process.

Please note that hot beeswax attracts bees, especially in spring.

I have had up to 20 bees in my studio on a warm spring morning, but they have never stung us or even been interested in us. If you are allergic or afraid, take the tin of hot wax to an area away from where you are working, and fill the design there, as the bees will stay with the wax. Bees are not active at night and very seldom on cloudy, cold or rainy days. Never leave the wax unattended while heating – it can ignite.

Other materials which may be used to fill in the back of a high-relief design are modelling paste and exterior crack filler. If using crack filler, add a water-based glue to the mixture. Fill the back of the pewter design with the filler, making sure the filler is level with the pewter. Clean off any excess crack filler with a damp cloth. Allow 24 hours to dry.

glass droppers

These are used to fill the back of the design with the beeswax. Glass droppers are inexpensive and easily available at pharmacies, so work with at least two or three. They will eventually clog up. When this happens, place the glass section into boiling water. Don't place the black rubber part into boiling water as it will perish; just pick out any cold wax with a tracer tool. Avoid turning the dropper upside down while it has hot wax in it, as the wax will run back and clog your dropper immediately.

degreaser

The front of the pewter must be free of any grease, otherwise the patina will not take. Always clean with a degreaser such as baby powder before starting the patina process. Do not worry about degreasing the back of the pewter. If you have excess lubricant on the back of the pewter, just wipe it off with a tissue. To degrease, place a little baby powder on cotton wool and gently rub over the design. Dishwashing liquid may also be used, but this will need to be rinsed off with clean water.

patina

Patina is a liquid, chemical substance which has a corrosive effect on metal. It is used on the pewter to give it an antique look. It also settles into the recesses of the design to give the design depth. The longer the patina is left on the pewter, the darker the pewter will become.

If you find the patina is too strong and darkens the pewter too much, dilute the patina with distilled water.

To apply patina, absorb a little on a small piece of cotton wool and wipe evenly over the pewter. When applying patina, wear protective gloves.

Patina does not have to be used if you do not like the effect. If your local craft shop does not stock patina, try a stained-glass shop or studio.

Be careful not to spill any patina onto your tools, as this will cause your tools to rust. If any spills occur, rinse off with clear water as this neutralises the effect of the patina.

metal polish

This is used to shine or buff up the metal, which enhances the design. Any household metal polish will work. Apply with a piece of cotton wool, then buff up using clean pieces of cotton wool. As soon as the piece of cotton wool being used becomes black, use another clean piece. Do not let the polish dry on the pewter as it becomes difficult to polish off. The harder you need to rub to remove the polish, the greater the risk that you may polish through the top tin-layer of the pewter.

Coal-stove polish (available at supermarkets) is lovely for experimenting. It will also darken the pewter and sit in the recesses of the design. Use it instead of the patina or apply it after the patina to enhance the effect.

modelling tools

Having the right tools makes it easier to achieve a professional finish. To do pewter you only need three specialized tools: a tracer, a paper pencil and a hockey-stick tool. Off course, having about three to five different sizes of ball tools as well, and both a large and a small hockey stick is ideal, but you can quite comfortably do pewter work with only three tools.

TRACER It is used to trace the design onto the pewter for high relief and low relief, and also to add the very fine detail to your design. The tracer has a rounded tip similar to that of a knitting needle or a ballpoint pen. A tool with a very small ball on the tip may also be used. The tracer must not be sharp, as it will cut through your pewter.

PAPER PENCIL Also known as a torchon, it is used to flatten and neaten the areas around the modelled design. As it is soft, it will leave no scratches. It is also used as a modelling tool for areas of the design for which the hockey stick is too large. The paper pencil is made of tightly-rolled paper (similar to a sucker stick) with a sharpened point at each end. To clean or sharpen the paper pencil, rub the sides of the point onto a piece of felt. After much use the paper pencil will need to be replaced, but the old, flattened one will make a good modelling tool. It's available at art shops as it's also used for blending chalk and oil pastels.

HOCKEY STICK It is used to model the pewter when doing high relief. If you are doing a very large design, a teaspoon can be used. Always keep the tool at a low angle. Only the middle, rounded part of the tool should touch the

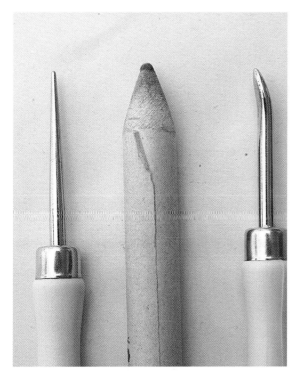

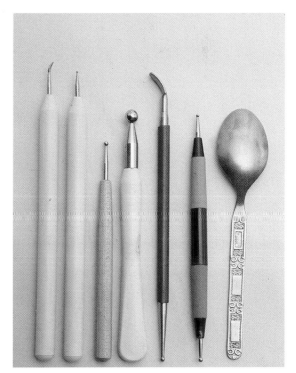

pewter; do not let the front point or sides touch as this will create grooves in your design. A small hockey stick is also available for modelling the small areas of the design. If you do not have one, a paper pencil may be used instead.

BALL TOOL The ball tool has a ball at the end of the tip and is available in various sizes. It is used when doing low relief to make a broader design line than the tracer will. It is also used to create raised dots or rounded areas on the pewter. When pushing out dots, be very careful not to push through the pewter. When wanting to broaden a design line, always start with the tracer and then use a larger ball tool. Never start with the larger ball tool, as pewter should be stretched out slowly or it will buckle.

glue

Any glue which is compatible with metal and the surface to which you are adhering the pewter will work. Ask at your hardware store. If you use anything other than water-based glue, clean off any excess with turpentine or vinegar. My glues of preference are non-water-based glue, contact glue and clear epoxy glue.

tracing paper

Use good quality tracing paper to transfer your designs. The thicker 60 gsm tracing paper is best. If you are working with thin tracing paper, the tracing tool will cut through it when you trace the design onto the pewter. This is very distracting and will cause the design to be traced unevenly.

rubber roller

This is used to flatten out the pewter sheet whenever necessary.

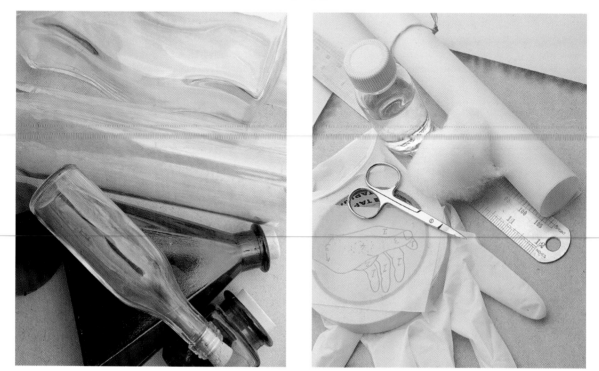

blanks

Undecorated boxes, clocks, bottles, frames, light-switch covers, tins etc. Decoupage blanks are particularly suitable. Make sure your base is fully prepared before attaching the pewter. All painting, sanding and varnishing must be done beforehand (see page 19).

miscellaneous requirements

Cotton wool to apply patina, to polish and for cleaning. This will be used in large quantities.

Masking tape to secure design to pewter while tracing.

Rubber or latex gloves to protect your hands when using patina.

Turpentine for cleaning off excess beeswax and glue.

Pencil and ruler.

Scissors. Small, curved nail scissors are best for cutting out designs.

Craft knife and cutting mat or glass surface.

Design & preparation

How do you find and create designs? Look! Look at everything. Pictures on wrapping paper, on greeting cards, in magazines, in design books, in children's books, photographs and so on. Printing has become very easy in the last two decades, so good printed material is easily available and just about everywhere. Any photograph or picture becomes a design once you have traced it into a line drawing. You can use more than one picture to create a scene. Some designs look attractive when repeated. This is very trendy right now.

Once your design has been sorted out, pay some attention to preparing the item to be decorated with pewter. Good preparation helps you to achieve a professional finish.

balancing a design

If you feel a design needs to be balanced to fit the space you are planning to cover with it, there are a number of things you can do. Have a look at the poppy book cover below. I placed the second leaf of the poppy away from the main flower. The reason for this is that once I had placed the poppy plant into the space, I felt the bottom right-hand area looked uncomfortably blank. I did not want to straighten the poppy stem, as I liked its soft, gentle curve. There are a number of other things I could have done. For example, I could have placed a smaller poppy flower or a little bug in that area. Or I could have created a label with the book's name on it. For this particular project I also textured the background, as I liked the contrast of the smooth, shinny poppy plant and the rougher background which holds more patina and polish. The more practical reason for the textured background is to prevent scratches showing on an item that is likely to be used often since it is a photograph album. I felt dents and scratches would not show as much as if I had left it plain.

tracing & line drawing

If the picture you have chosen is not the right size for your project, trace it to create a line drawing and then size the line drawing rather than the original picture on a photocopy machine.

low relief & high relief

Once you have created your design, you will need to decide which part of the design will be in low relief and which part in high relief – which section will be at the highest level and which section at the lowest level once modelled. To make your modelling easier, especially if you are still a novice,

indicate this on your design by using numbers, for instance (see Sculptured hand, page 32).

using stencils

This is a really easy way to use designs without even having to trace them onto tracing paper. Apply stencil glue to the back of the stencil, or spray with spray glue. Allow a few minutes for the glue to get tacky. Secure the pewter to hard board with masking tape and place the stencil onto the pewter. You will not need to stick it down with masking tape as the glue will keep the stencil securely in position.

Using the tracing tool, trace the design onto the pewter. Remove the stencil and continue your relief modelling.

CRAFTERS NOTE
If the stencil you want to use is the wrong size, trace the design onto tracing paper and size it on a photocopy machine. Now simply trace the line-drawing onto the pewter.

preparing superwood blanks

Superwood decoupage blanks will provide you with endless good ideas for pewter projects. Several projects in this book are done on these, namely the clock, tissue box and mirror set, jewellery box and picture frames, both large and small. The blanks are inexpensive and available at all craft and decoupage shops. They are easy to prepare: all you need are a sponge applicator or paint brush, 400-grit sandpaper, water-based or acrylic paint in a colour of your choice and water-based varnish.

First unscrew all hinges and clasps. Using a sponge applicator or paintbrush, paint your item with a water-based or acrylic

paint in a colour of your choice (see Crafters notes below if you want a wood finish). Leave to dry. The box now feels very rough, so sand it with 400-grit sandpaper. If there are routed edges on your item, spend some time making sure they are well sanded. Thoroughly wipe away all wood dust.

Repaint the item with enough coats to cover it well. Allow to dry between coats. To finish off, apply two coats of water-based varnish. Most makes of varnish come in matt, satin and gloss. The choice is yours.

Replace all the hinges and clasps. Your box is now ready to have the pewter work glued to it.

CRAFTERS NOTES
• If you want a wood finish to your item, prepare with a wood varnish, available at hardware stores. You may add a stain to the varnish to create the wood colour you require. Prepare the box as above, using wood varnish instead of the water based paint. The tissue box and mirror on page 68 have been prepared with wood varnish.
• For a professional finish, I always cut out and stick a piece of cork sheeting to the bottom of my boxes and flat-bottomed items. The cork is available from most craft and hardware shops.

General hints & tips

Having done pewter relief-modelling for many years, I have discovered shortcuts and easy solutions to several challenges. Using these may help make your pewter experience a fun one. You may discover many of your own shortcuts and solutions along the way.

using a pattern tracer

A pattern tracer, which is a very inexpensive sewing tool and available from all sewing shops, makes a great tool for pewter work. Run it along a ruler to create a line of little dots. This makes interesting borders.

metric circle-template

Another handy tool to own is a metric circle-template. It is a stencil with about 30 different sized circles. I use this whenever I need a circle, for suitcase corners, for patterns with circles and for rounding corners on borders.

positioning your design

Before gluing your pewter design onto your object of choice, stick it on with double-sided tape to make sure the position and angle are correct.

accidentally piercing the pewter

If you accidentally push through the pewter while doing high relief, don't panic, all is not lost. When filling the design with beeswax some of the wax will run through the hole, but it will solidify and thereby close the hole. Once you have filled the back with wax and cleaned off any excess wax with turps, turn the design over and gently clean the wax from the front as well. Very carefully press back bits of pewter that are out of place – they will stick to the wax and no one will ever notice. Patina and polish as usual. The higher the pewter design is modelled the thinner the pewter becomes, as it has been stretched. This is when you need to work very carefully with any ball tool or tracer to avoid accidents like this.

balsa wood

This is a good option for cutting out shapes you cannot find in the shops. You can use it for the

Christmas bauble (see page 83) and the pendant (see page 78). It is a soft, light wood, usually used for model aeroplanes. It is available at art and hobby shops and you can cut it with a sharp craft knife. As long your balsa wood is at least 5 mm thick, it will not warp. If you need to paint it, seal it first with sanding sealer available at hardware stores.

photocopy designs onto tracing paper

To avoid having to trace intricate designs twice (once onto the tracing paper and once onto the pewter), photocopy them onto the tracing paper and then trace them onto the pewter. This will save you time and frustration. If you do not have access to a sophisticated photocopy machine make sure you are using 60 gsm tracing paper. This is quite thick and will not jam the machine.

simple safety precautions

Pewter contains lead, therefore you should be careful when working with this metal. Always wash your hands after you've worked with it, don't rub your eyes while working with it, and keep your hands away from your mouth. Do not use pewter to decorate items that will be used to serve food.

use punched shapes

Craft punches work well with pewter, a very soft metal that will not blunt the blade any quicker than paper card will. This adds a whole range of shapes for cards and scrapbook pages. Applying patina and polish to these small shapes will test your fine motor skills. You may want to omit this process, or do it before punching out the shapes. I traced the veins onto the punched shapes and then applied patina and polish. Don't use punches on copper sheeting.

Basic techniques

By completing three beginner's projects you will learn to master the basic techniques used in pewter work, namely low-relief and high-relief modelling.

As these are the only two techniques used when doing pewter work, spend some time practising them before moving on to more challenging designs. It will be worth it, saving you lots of frustrating moments and wasted pieces of pewter. Once you have mastered the two techniques of low relief and high relief, there is not much you cannot achieve with pewter modelling. Use the beginner's projects as your reference to refresh your memory if necessary when you are doing other projects.

Before you start, a general observation on modelling pressure. Some people are heavy-handed, some light-handed. You will need to discover you ideal pressure yourself. Until you find your correct pressure, rather err on the side of caution – be light-handed. You can always go back to achieve a deeper indentation, but once you've pierced the pewter, it's pierced (see General hints and tips page 20).

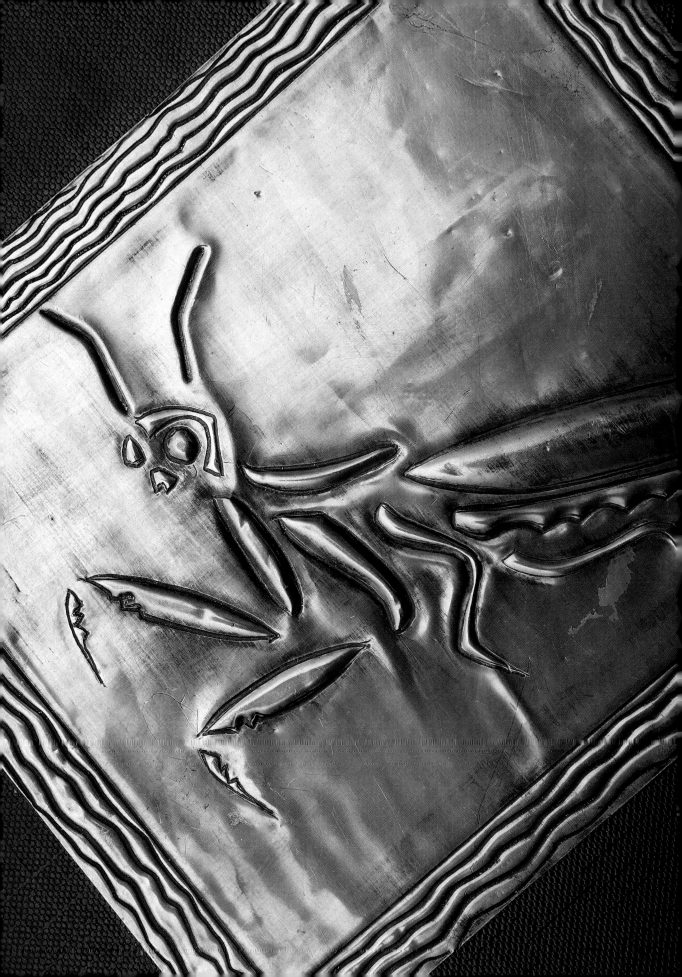

Low-relief greeting card

If you are a novice, it is really important that you start with this project. Resist the urge to jump ahead. It is a good idea at this point to re read the section on tools (see pages 8-15). I have designed this project to cover only low-relief modelling, so you can gain an understanding of this technique before combining it with high-relief modelling. With low-relief modelling no filling from the back is required.

you will need

smooth, hard board for work
   surface
soft cloth or felt
design on page 119 traced onto
   tracing paper
piece of pewter just larger than
   design
masking tape
tracer tool
ruler
paper pencil
small ball-tool (optional)
small rubber-roller (optional)
degreaser
cotton wool
rubber or latex gloves
patina
household metal polish
blank greeting card
glue
piece of textured paper

1. Place the cloth on the hard board. Place pewter right side up on the single cloth and secure with masking tape. *(Note: The right side has a whitish tint, the wrong side a bluish tint. If you are unsure, test using patina on a small piece of pewter; the patina will not take on the wrong side.)* Centre the traced design onto the pewter with masking tape.

2. Using the tracer tool, trace the straight lines using the ruler to

guide you. Press just a little harder than writing pressure. Trace the rest of the design, excluding the dots. Remove the tracing paper and all masking tape.

3. Place the pewter on the hard board, right side up. Neaten up your work by rubbing with a flat finger over the traced design, or, using a small rubber roller, gently roll over designs to flatten. *(Note: You always neaten up your work on the hard board. If you neaten up on*

the soft cloth, you will buckle the pewter.)

4. Return the pewter to the cloth, right side up. If your design has not indented as much as you would like it to, retrace the design lines with the tracer, pressing a little harder. Place the pewter on the hard board, right side up, and neaten up your work by rubbing over it with a flat finger or using a rubber roller.

5. Place pewter wrong side up on the hard board. Using the paper pencil, trace on either side of the raised lines of the heart. This will

neaten and sharpen the line of the heart. Repeat this step for the rest of the design, the flower and the two spirals.

6. Place the pewter wrong side up on the cloth. Using the tracer or small ball-tool, lightly press

dots around the inside of the rectangle. Do not press too hard when you do this, as you can push through the pewter. (*Note: The ball tool will give you larger dots than the tracer tool.*)

7.   Return the pewter, right side up, to the hard board. Neaten by rubbing with a flat finger or rolling with the rubber roller. Degrease the right side of the pewter by rubbing cotton wool dipped into baby powder over the pewter to remove all grease. The pressure of rubbing should be firm, but not hard. You do not want to remove the top shiny layer of tin. (*Note: The patina will not take where there is grease.*)

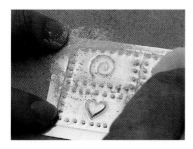

8.   Wearing rubber or latex gloves, absorb a little patina onto a small piece of cotton wool and apply evenly over the pewter. (*Note: It is safer to pour a little patina into a shallow receptacle such as a small yoghurt cup and dipping the cotton wool into it, rather than placing*

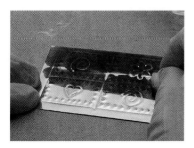

cotton wool over the open bottle and tipping the bottle over.) Rinse off under cold running tap and pat dry with tissue. Degrease again to remove residue from the patina.

9.   Place the pewter right side up on the hard board. Absorb a little metal polish onto cotton wool and rub over the pewter. Using clean cotton wool, gently buff to remove excess polish. Do not rub too hard and replace cotton wool as soon as the piece you are using becomes black. You will use a lot of cotton wool. (*Note: If the metal polish becomes dry, apply fresh polish and buff. This will remove the dry polish.*)

10. Cut out your design with decorative scissors (see page 38) and stick onto a greeting card. I used a backing as well as a piece of textured paper for interest.

CRAFTERS NOTES
• In this project you have worked on the right side and the wrong side of the pewter. When doing low relief you may work from either side. If you impress your design on the right side, the design will be indented; it will also hold more patina and polish and therefore become blacker. If you impress your design from the wrong side, the design will be slightly raised (not high relief), it will not hold patina and polish and will therefore be shiny. You make these choices when deciding on the design of your project. The contrast of the two gives interest to the design.

• When doing your low relief from the back of the pewter, remember the design will be in mirror image on the front. This is particularly important to remember when doing numbers or letters of the alphabet.

• Although this is the simpler of the techniques it can be very effective used on its own without the contrast of high relief.

• If you battle initially with the right and wrong side of the pewter, mark the back with a permanent marker (press lightly) so that you do not get confused when following the right-side-up and wrong-side-up instructions.

• If you want to 'fatten' the straight lines of the design, use a small to medium-sized ball-tool instead of the tracer in step 4.

• If you find you are very heavy handed, use a mouse pad or self-healing cutting mat instead of a soft cloth when tracing your design.

High-relief butterfly

The high-relief technique is the one most people find exciting. It is a step-by-step process, so use the notes of this project whenever you are doing a high-relief design, the process does not change. Do not despair that you need to constantly refer back to the notes, it does not matter at all. Once you have worked on a lot of pewter designs you will find that it becomes second nature, just like driving a car. When doing any high-relief project concentrate on the shape of the sculptured design rather than on pushing the pewter out as far as it can go.

you will need

design on page 119 traced onto
  tracing paper
smooth board for work surface
piece of pewter just larger than
  design
masking tape
2 layers of soft cloth or felt
tracer tool
lubricant such as petroleum jelly
hockey-stick tool
paper pencil
small ball-tool (optional)
beeswax and glass dropper
degreaser
cotton wool
patina
rubber or latex gloves
turpentine
household metal-polish
blank greeting card
piece of textured paper
glue

1. Place the pewter right side up onto the smooth, hard board and secure with masking tape. Place traced design onto pewter, securing well with masking tape. Trace the design onto the pewter using the tracer tool. Press a little harder than writing pressure. *(Note: You complete this step on the hard board, not on the soft cloth, because at this stage you are only to transferring your design onto the pewter; you are not yet modelling the design.)*

2. Remove the tracing paper and turn the pewter over, wrong side up, onto the hard board. Lubricate the back of the pewter with a little petroleum jelly or any other lubricant. Place the pewter, still wrong side up, onto a double layer of felt.

3. Imagine the butterfly is divided into five parts: four wings and a body. Work each part separately. The outline of the design which surrounds the separate parts, namely the wings and the body, will remain at surface level. Do not model over these lines. Using the hockey-stick modelling tool, start in the centre of the first wing and very gently and softly work the tool over the pewter in a gentle circular motion, remaining inside the lines of the wing. Model each of the four wings. At this stage ignore the inner wing detail of the two top wings just continue to model over them as if they were not there. (*Note: Most people automatically hold the hockey stick is as they would hold a pen. This is wrong as it turns the tool onto its pointy nose. Hold the tool as you would hold a fork if you were shovelling food into your mouth (see picture). Never let the nose or the sides of the tool touch the pewter, as this will cause grooves.*)

4. Model the body using the paper pencil, as the hockey stick is too large for this small area. Do not model too deep, as this will cause pewter to buckle.

5. Turn pewter over (right side up), place on hard board and trace around the design with the paper pencil, staying on the design lines which will remain at surface level, around the body and each of the four wings. This is done to neaten up the design. Continue to ignore the inner detail on the top wings. (*Note: A common mistake at this stage is forgetting to place the pewter on the hard board. If you start tracing around the design while it is on the cloth you will indent the pewter on the outside of the butterfly where it must remain flat.*)

6. Repeat steps 3 to 5 as many times as necessary to create the depth of relief you want. (*Note: It is very important not to rush these three steps. Work your modelling slowly so the pewter does not buckle, as you cannot fix it once it has buckled.*) When you are satisfied with the size and shape of your butterfly, turn the pewter over, wrong side up, and place onto a double layer of felt. You are ready to do the second level of the design.

7. Model the small inner-wing detail using a paper pencil as the hockey stick is too big. (*Note: If the wing detail is not stretching out, place the work onto a triple layer of felt, to give the pewter a softer surface into which it can be moulded.*)

8. Place the pewter right side up onto the hard board and gently trace around the butterfly's wings and body with the tracer or a small ball-tool. Trace around all lines except the feelers and inner wing detail. Keep exactly on the original design lines so you do not create double lines. This gives your design a crisp finish.

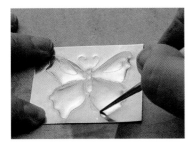

9. Place the pewter right side up onto a single layer of felt and retrace the feelers with the tracer or small ball-tool (low relief).

10. Turn the pewter wrong side up, melt the beeswax and fill the back of the design using the glass dropper. (*Note: If the beeswax is hardening in the dropper it is not hot enough.*) Allow to harden.

11. Place pewter wrong side up on a cloth to prevent the front from scratching. Make sure all areas are filled with wax which should be level with the edge of the design. Clean off excess beeswax with turpentine on cotton wool. Replace cotton wool when the piece being used is full of wax.

12. Place the pewter right side up on the hard board. Using the tracer, gently trace the horizontal

body segment lines, and around the inner wing detail to define it.

13. Degrease the front of design using cotton wool dipped into baby powder. Rub gently over pewter. Wearing rubber or latex gloves, absorb a little patina onto cotton wool and apply evenly over the pewter. Rinse off in water pat dry with a tissue. Degrease again to remove residue from patina. Polish with metal polish and cotton wool.

14. Cut out your design with decorative scissors (see page 38) and stick onto a greeting card. I used a backing as well as a piece of textured paper for interest.

CRAFTERS NOTE

The slower you sculpture your design from the back, in other words the more times you repeat steps 3 to 5, the more control you will have of the final relief shape. You need to see it grow slowly so you can decide which areas need to be modelled more deeply. This is how your picture takes shape. Not all parts of the picture will be the same height. Once you have stretched the pewter out too far there is no way of reversing the process.

Sculptured hand

This is the last beginners project. I have designed it specifically to help you pactise the sculpturing of high relief. Although most good quality pewter will give you a lot of height, the ideal is to create the correct sculptured shape, not the highest relief shape. I found once I had mastered low and high relief and I started doing more intricate designs, the challenge was to do the various sections of my design at the right height in order to achieve the most pleasing result. I have numbered the various levels of height on this design (see page 34) with number 1 being the lowest level.

you will need

design on page 119 traced onto
    tracing paper
smooth board for work surface
piece of pewter just larger than
    design
masking tape
2 layers of soft cloth or felt
tracer tool
lubricant such as petroleum jelly
hockey-stick tool
paper pencil
beeswax and glass dropper
degreaser
cotton wool
patina
rubber or latex gloves
turpentine
household metal-polish
glue
small tin

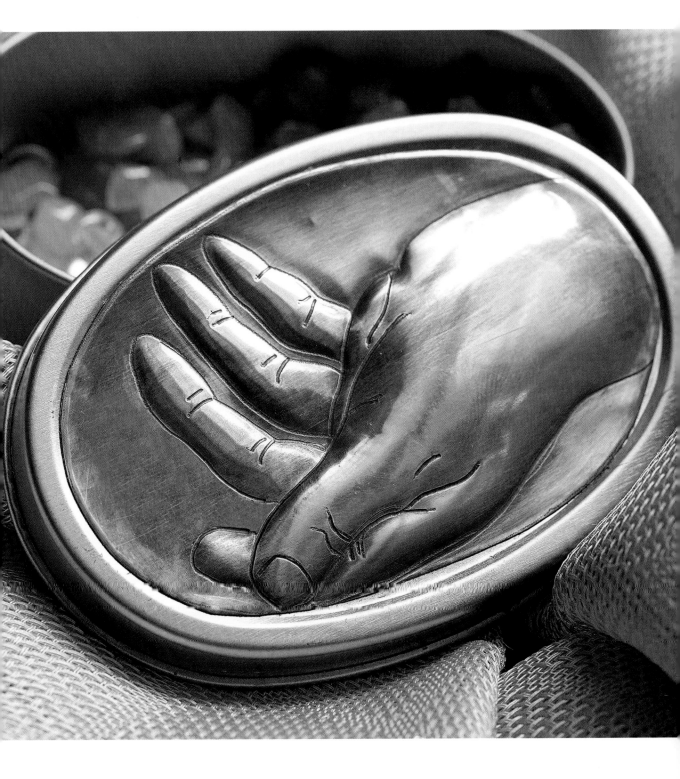

1. Place the pewter right side up onto the hard board and secure with masking tape. Place traced design onto pewter, securing well with masking tape. Trace the design onto the pewter using the tracer tool.

2. Remove the tracing paper and turn the pewter over, wrong side up, onto hard board. Lubricate the back with petroleum jelly and place pewter, still wrong side up, onto a double layer of felt.

3. Using the hockey stick, gently model each of the four fingers. Work each finger separately. Using a teaspoon, holding it like you would hold the hockey stick, gently model the rest of hand and thumb. Pay no attention to the finger-creases or the thumbnail outline, at this stage. These will be done after you have placed the beeswax. *(Note: Do not press too hard or model too deeply.)*

4. Turn the pewter over, right side up, onto hard board. Trace around the design with the paper pencil, staying on the lines of the design. Trace around the outline, between the four fingers and the line at the bottom of the pinkie and ring finger. All these lines remain at surface level. Do not trace around the outline of the thumb as it is raised. Repeat steps 3 and 4 until all parts of the design are at the height you want level 1 to be.

5. Place pewter wrong side up onto a double layer of cloth. Using the paper pencil, model the little area of flesh below the pinkie and ring finger in high relief. Using the teaspoon, gently model all other areas of the hand until they are all at the same height. This is level 2. Do not model any areas marked 1 as you have completed level 1. Turn the pewter over, right side up, and neaten up by

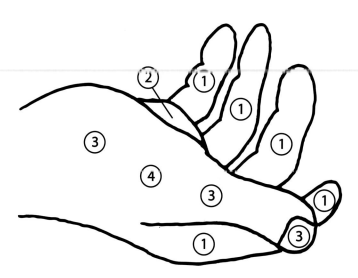

tracing around the design with the paper pencil. (*Note: Trace around the complete design, including areas marked 1.*) You have now completed the second level.

6. Place the pewter wrong side up onto a double layer of cloth. Using the teaspoon, model the remaining areas in high relief the height of level 3. Turn the pewter over, right side up, and trace around the complete design with the paper pencil. Repeat the entire process to model the area marked 4 until it is just higher than level 3.

7. If you are happy with the sculpture of the hand, place the pewter right side up on the hard board and trace around the de-

sign with the paper pencil, then trace around the design with a tracer or small ball tool to do the final neatening up of the design. The thumbnail and finger creases will be done after the beeswax, but before the patina.

8. Turn the pewter wrong side up, melt the beeswax and fill the back of the design using the glass dropper. Wipe off any excess

beeswax with turpentine.

9. Place design right side up onto the hard board. Using the tracer, trace all finger creases, the thumbnail outline, and the outline of the thumb. Use a little pressure, as you want to create a slight impression into the pewter.

10. Degrease the front of the design, patina and polish. Cut to size and glue onto a tin.

CRAFTERS NOTE
What you have done here is to model your entire design to level 1, then level 2, then level 3 and so on. All pewter relief-modelling should be completed this way. It does not work to push out the highest level first, as this will become flattened as you then work on the lower levels. Use the numbering system on you tracing paper if it helps you. It is a very good way to plan your design. The card with the nude bust (see page 104) was done in exactly the same way.

Accompanying techniques

Once you have mastered low relief, high relief and sculpturing (using different levels of high relief), there are some accompanying techniques that will enable you to create a wide variety of pewter-decorated items.

Many pewter designs are cut out and glued to an item to be decorated, sometimes paper patterns can be used for accurate pewter work, in some instances colour is added, you may want to use texture, decorative borders or edging, or you may want to add corners to finish off your design. These techniques are all dealt with here.

Cutting out pewter designs

Cutting out your design neatly is very important as a poor cutting job can spoil your work and detract from an overall pleasing look. Complete your pewter design, including the entire patina and polishing process before cutting out. If applicable, make sure all excess beeswax has been cleaned from the back of the pewter.

A pair of curved cuticle scissors works best for cutting out pewter designs, although a pair of small pointed scissors may also be used. When cutting out with the cuticle scissors, have the curve facing away from the area of the design you are cutting out.

Use a craft knife or scalpel for those awkward areas you cannot reach with a pair of scissors. If you are handy with a swivel-blade craft knife this also works well. Whatever your choice, always make sure your blade is sharp.

When cutting out with a blade or knife the best surface to work on is a self-healing cutting mat. It will not blunt your blade, which glides smoothly over the mat, giving you total control of direction. The lines on the cutting mat will also help you to cut straight edges if you line up a steel ruler with the lines and then cut along the ruler with a craft knife. Cutting mats are available from all art and craft shops. A small A4 size is all you need. A piece of glass will also work, but is harsher on your blades and does not have the useful guidelines of a cutting mat.

Square and rectangular designs for bottles, cards, gift-bags and scrapbook pages can also be cut out with decorative scissors.

Paper patterns

When covering items with pewter, it is necessary to have a pattern of the object you wish to cover in order to cut out the correct shape of pewter. This minimizes pewter waste and irritation and helps you achieve a neat, professional finish. Use paper templates to figure out how to achieve the process of covering the object. Should you for example bend the pewter around the corners, or should you work each side separately? Practise with paper so by the time you come to cover the item with your precious artwork you know exactly how to go about it. I will take you through covering a business-card holder, which has a tricky, ornate shape at the back. I covered the three sides of the box with one long piece of pewter which is folded around the corners.

you will need

business-card holder
tracing paper
ruler
pencil
design
craft knife or scissors
masking tape
glue

1. Paint and prepare the business-card holder (see page 19).

2. Place the business-card holder onto the tracing paper and draw around it.

3. Cut out the paper pattern. Cut the paper pattern to fit inside the card holder. (*Note: Don't worry if the pattern is slightly taller than the box; you can trim this to fit exactly when the pewter has been stuck onto the box.*)

4. Measure and draw the front and sides of the box and cut out the pattern.

5. Trace your designs onto the paper pattern.

6. Using your paper pattern, cut out the pewter. Secure the tracing paper pattern onto the pewter and trace the designs onto the pewter as detailed in the beginner's projects. Complete design as desired. Patina and polish.

7. Glue the pewter onto the business-card holder and carefully trim off any excess pewter using a craft knife.

CRAFTERS NOTES
• You may find it easier to cut out the pewter if the pattern is secured with masking tape.
• I painted the card holder with black water-based craft paint and then polished the paint with black coal-stove polish for a really attractive metallic finish.

Adding corners

These simple corners, like the ones which were used on the rectangular school-suitcases of old, are a great way to balance the pewter on a box project. Unadorned, they are very elegant and will not detract from the design on the top or lid.

The quill of the guinea-fowl feather in this project (see design on page 126) is done in high relief. The rest of the feather is done in low relief. The spots are metal leaf. I placed the pewter onto a cutting mat when doing the low relief, as I did not want it to indent too deeply. The cutting mat gives more support than a single layer of felt, resulting in a shallower indentation.

you will need

wooden box
pewter
metric-circle tool
scissors
degreaser
patina
household metal-polish
glue

1. Cut out 4 circles of pewter. Patina and polish the circles. Mark the centre of each circle with a khoki. Make a cut from the edge of the circle to the centre.

2. Turn the box upside down. Place onto a soft cloth to prevent the top of the box from scratching. Apply glue to the back of the pewter circle. Place the centre of the pewter circle on the corner of the box with the cut pointing straight up.

3. Fold the right flap down onto the bottom of the box.

4. Fold the left flap over the right flap.

5. Repeat for the other corners.

CRAFTER'S NOTES
• Experiment first by cutting out a few paper circles in varying sizes and folding them around the corners to determine the right size for your box.
• If you are going to adhere cork sheeting to the underside of the box, do this after the corners have been placed.

Textures and backgrounds

Textures add interest and contrast to pewter work and often complete the picture, for example the wood grain on the chameleon's branch (see page 49). The different patterns will reflect light differently and set the various sections of the design apart. There are a number of patterns you can use, for example cross hatching, slanted and straight lines, dots, zigzags, circles and twirls. A textured background will set off the smoothness of high relief. You can also texture the high relief, for example the scales of the lizards on the pottery planter (see page 98).

frames & borders

As part of your design you may create a frame or border around your picture. Using a pair of deckle edge or decorative craft scissors will give a charming finish to your design. The cookie-cup birthday card on page 103 is a good example.

patterns

I have used various textured patterns on the designs of the orange candles (see page 92-93). The bark of the palm trees have a linier low-relief design which contrasts with the smooth background and the smooth horizontal sections of the trunk. It also holds more patina and polish and is therefore darker. The different patterns on the hill lines introduce interest and contrast, which set them apart from the background and each other. To create these textures use a combination of indented low relief and raised low relief. The indented low relief will hold more black.

texturing after beeswax

Create indented low relief on the high relief design by using a tracer or small ball tool. Do this after the beeswax has been placed in the back of the design, but before doing the patina and polishing. I used this method to create the patterns on the hill lines, the veins of the leaves and the fur on the cat.

raised patterns

To create raised patterns on the high-relief design, first complete the high relief – in other words take it out to its highest level. Place the pewter wrong side up onto a soft cloth. Very carefully push out the pattern using a small ball-tool. The pewter has already been stretched and is therefore thin, so it is very easy to push through the pewter at this point. Fill with beeswax and polish.

Adding colour

There are a number of interesting ways to colour pewter. Gilding or metal leafing is the most popular, but using glass paints, glitter or acrylic paints are also fun ways to create texture and add non-metallic colours. Once again, use your imagination and experiment.

The patina and polishing process of your project must be complete before any colour is added to the pewter. If you are covering an item with pewter it is also best to do any colouring after the item has been covered.

Gilding

True gold leaf is very expensive and not readily available. Take heart, though, as we use the far less expensive alternative known as metal leaf. This is available in various colours at art and craft shops. It is sold in book form. The fine metal-leaf sheets are placed between sheets of tissue paper. When cutting the metal leaf, cut it with a piece of the protective tissue paper.

Lightly dust your hands with powder while working with metal leaf as perspiration from your hands may cause oxidization which will spoil the finish.

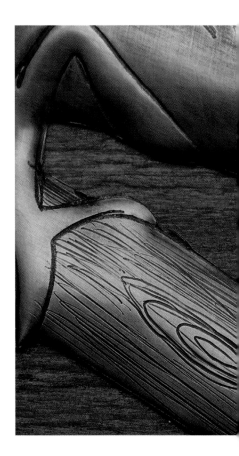

you will need

shellac (blond) – thin flakes of a
   resinous substance used to make
   varnish
methylated or white spirits
old stocking
small piece of cotton wool
gold-leaf glue
small, inexpensive paintbrush
talcum powder for dusting hands
sheets of metal leaf
small, sharp pair of scissors
acetone for cleaning brush used to
   apply shellac

1. Mix shellac crystals with methylated or white spirits to form a varnish. It should have the same consistency as normal wood varnish.

2. Cut a piece of stocking about 16 cm long, place a cotton wool ball inside and tie the stocking into a knot. This will be used as your 'sandpaper'.

4. Leave the glue to dry for about 15 minutes. The glue dries clear. Do not place the metal leaf over the glue if the glue is still milky – it will not stick.

5. Powder your hands. Cut out pieces of metal leaf and place over the glue. The pieces of metal leaf do not have to be cut out the exact size and shape of the area to be gilded as you can overlap the pieces of metal leaf to cover the glued area. Press down firmly.

6. Gently rub the stocking-covered cotton wool over your design. This will buff away all excess pieces of metal leaf and leave the gilding smooth. Collect excess metal leaf and store for future use. Leave for about one hour to dry.

6. Paint the shellac over the gilded area and clean the brush with acetone.

CRAFTERS NOTES

• Mix up a lot more shellac than needed and keep in a screw top bottle ready for use.

• If gold is not your colour, shop around for silver or copper metal leaf. Some shops stock only the gold but many do stock other colours.

• Try polishing the gold leaf with black coal stove polish before varnishing. This will give it an interesting antique look (see jewellery box on page 70).

• The stocking-covered cotton wool also makes a great tool for buffing up the pewter.

3. Using the paintbrush, paint all areas you wish to gild with the gold-leaf glue, taking care not to spill any glue on areas you do not wish to gild.

Glitter

When designing fairies for little girls, they just have to have glitter, glitter and more glitter. So if you want to please a fairy soul, best you know how to glitter your pewter. I used gold powder on the fairy wings, rainbow glitter for her wand and shoes, and magenta glitter for the mushroom. Once again, the glitter is added as a final finish after the pewter work has been completed.

you will need

various colours and textures of
  glitter
shellac (see Gilding on page 48)
small inexpensive paintbrush
acetone for cleaning shellac off
  brush

1. Paint shellac onto the area you wish to glitter. Work on one area at a time so you can control where the glitter sticks. Pour enough glitter onto the wet shellac to cover the area well. Shake off excess glitter onto a piece of paper. Using the paper as a funnel, pour glitter back into bottle.

2. Repeat until all desired areas have been covered with glitter. Leave to dry, about 30 minutes. Paint shellac over all areas covered with glitter. This will seal and therefore protect the glitter. You will, however, still be able to feel the texture of the glitter.

Paint

Glass paint is available in many wonderful rich colours. It has a translucent, high-gloss finish, which gives glass-painted surfaces a gorgeous jewel look when light is reflected off them. Glass paint works well on metal because it is designed to adhere to a non-absorbent surface and therefore does not need to be varnished. A simple low-relief design can really be brought to life with these paints.

Acrylic paint can be used with equal success to embellish pewter work. Simply apply the acrylic paint to the required area using a soft paintbrush. Once the paint has dried, apply a coat of shellac or any water-based varnish over the painted area to prevent the paint being scratched off.

you will need

glass paints

small, soft paintbrush

acetone for cleaning paintbrush

Simply apply the glass paint to the desired areas with a small soft paintbrush. The glass paint is designed to fill in areas between liquid lead, so works best if the area around it is raised, like the border of the heart as shown here on the teapot design for a tea tin.

CRAFTERS NOTE

• Use acetone to thin down glass paint or to clean your brush after applying glass paint.

• Because acrylic paints are made for absorbent surfaces such as paper, you will find they scratch off the pewter very easily. Once protected with varnish, this will not happen.

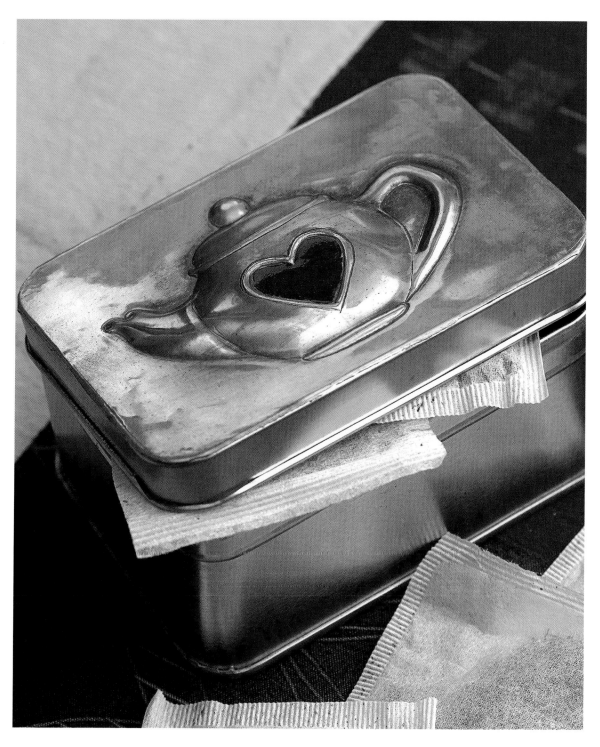

Covered items

Because pewter is so soft and can be moulded, it is ideal to cover various blanks, an ideal way to instantly create what looks like an ancient heirloom.

Until they actually pick them up and realize how light they are, few people realize that the jewellery boxes on pages 70 and 72 and the antique clock on page 74, for example, are simply wooden decoupage blanks covered with a pewter-work design.

Light-switch cover

These are very popular. Replacing an ordinary cream light-switch cover with a gorgeous pewter one will transform any room. The challenge when placing a design on a light-switch cover is that the design must fit around the various screw and switch holes, and preferably incorporate them. It does not work to have a screw placed in an inappropriate area of the design. All of this must be factored into your design. I positioned the dragonfly's body so that the screw would form one of its segments (see photograph on page 59). The screws also make good flower centres.

you will need

removable light-switch cover

tracing paper

design on page 127 or 124 (or your own suitable design)

pencil

pewter 1 cm bigger all round than light-switch cover

tracer and modelling tools

bees wax and dropper

patina

cotton wool

household metal-polish

scissors

soft cloth

smooth, hard board

sharp knife

glue

1. Place the light-switch cover face down onto the tracing paper. Trace around the cover, as well as all screw holes and switch opening. Place the tracing of the light-switch cover over your chosen design, making sure it is not affected by any of the screw holes or the switch opening, or that these can be incorporated in the design, and trace the design onto the tracing paper. Trace the design onto pewter. Trace the rectangular shape of the switch opening onto the pewter. Don't trace the outer edge of the cover or the screw holes. *(Note: While working on your design, ignore the rectangular shape of the switch.)*

2. Complete your pewter design including the filling, patina and polishing processes.

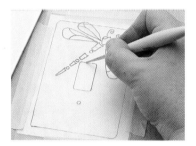

3. Apply glue to the back of the pewter, placing it over the front of the light switch cover. Line up the switch opening of the cover with the traced switch opening on the pewter.

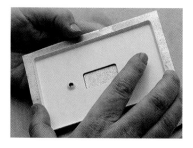

4. Cut off any excess pewter at the corners.

5. Place the pewter face down on a soft cloth so that it does not get scratched. Carefully fold the edges of the pewter over the

metal cover, making sure that the switch opening on the cover and the traced switch rectangle on the pewter stay lined up.

6. Run the rounded back of a tool along the inside edge of the light-switch cover to stick the pewter down neatly.

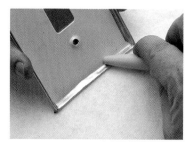

7. Carefully roll the pewtered corners of the light-switch cover on the soft cloth to mould them over the corners of the cover. Press down on the inside of the cover.

8. Place the light-switch cover onto a self-healing cutting mat or onto the soft cloth. The wrong side of the light-switch cover must be facing up. Using a sharp craft knife cut an X into the pewter

at the switch opening. Cut from corner to corner.

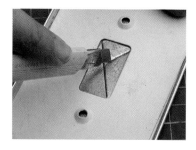

9. Press a finger into the X from the right side of the cover, so you are pushing the pewter through to the wrong side. Press the pewter down on the wrong side.

10. You may need to trim the pewter to fit underneath the screw holes.

11. Using your tracer, gently press the screw holes from the back. Press just hard enough to make indentations on the front to mark where the screw holes will be.

12. Turn the cover over. Place the point of the tracer on the screw-hole marks and press back to create the holes. Place the light-switch cover proudly onto the wall.

CRAFTERS NOTES
• By adding 1 cm all round to the measurement of the light-switch cover you will be sure there is enough pewter to wrap around the sides of the light switch cover.
• The easiest thing to do is to cover your existing covers. This will be necessary if the covers in your home are not standard. Many of the light-switch covers in old houses are no longer available in stores.

Frames

Superwood frames are freely available at all hobby, craft and art shops. They come in various sizes and shapes. You can cover the frame with pewter or you may paint the frame and glue a cut-out design onto the painted frame. Ready-to-use frames are also great for decorating with your own pewter touch. Look around at the home stores – they have a lovely variety of frames at reasonable prices.

Both these frames are superwood frames, which have been covered with pewter. The design on page 124 has been adapted to fit the smaller frame. The shiny triangles and the raised circles in the corners have been completed in high relief. The darker triangles are not raised but have been textured with low relief. I placed the design right side up onto a single cloth and completed the low relief using the tracer tool. I made thin parallel lines very close together. The rough texture of the low relief contrasts well with the smooth texture of the high relief. The parallel lines which run above and below the triangles were modelled in low relief and were indented from the front.

On the large frame I left the areas between the two rows of triangles flat and untextured. I repeated this between the row of triangles and the photograph, but added a raised, linear border around the photograph.

On the smaller frame I textured the area between the row of triangles and the photograph area with cross-hatching. This was done using the tracer and indenting the pewter from the front.

The design of these two frames is very mathematical and repetitive. The contrast of the smooth high relief and very textured low relief give the design a lot of interest. The high, smooth triangles catch the light, while the darker textured triangles appear to recede, making the high relief triangles the area that catches the eye.

you will need

frame
tracing paper
design on page 124 (or your own
  suitable design)
pencil
pewter
tracer and modelling tools
beeswax and dropper
patina
cotton wool
household metal-polish
glue
scissors
soft cloth
smooth, hard board
craft knife and cutting mat

1. Prepare your frame as you would a wooden box (see page 19). The front of the frame does not need to be painted, as it will not be seen once covered. The sides and back must be properly prepared.

2. Measure your frame and add 1 cm plus the measurement of the thickness of the frame to all four sides to allow for the overlap at the back. Cut a piece of pewter this size. My frame measures 10 x 10 cm. I added 1 cm for the overlap, plus 0,5 cm for the thickness of the frame to each side. My pewter measured 13 x 13 cm.

3. Place the frame face down onto tracing paper, trace around the inside and outside of the frame. Trace your design onto

this pattern, then trace the design onto the pewter. Complete your pewter work, fill with beeswax and complete the patina and polishing processes.

4. Apply glue to the back of the pewter and position it onto the face of the frame. Make sure your design is lined up with the frame. Place the frame and pewter wrong side up onto a cutting mat, working carefully to avoid scratching the design.

5. Make a cut extending from the corner of the wooden frame to the corner of the pewter.

6. Cut the corner off the pewter. (Note: The distance from the wooden frame corner to where you cut off the pewter corner, is the same

measurement as the thickness of your frame. For example, the thickness of my frame is 0,5 cm. My pewter corner is cut 0,5 cm away from the wooden frame corner.) Repeat this step for the remaining three corners.

7. Fold one side of pewter over the frame.

8. Fold down the little flap which is still standing up.

9. Fold the next side of pewter over the frame and fold over the little flap which is still standing up. Repeat for the other corners.

10. Cut out the centre piece of pewter leaving a 1,5 cm pewter edge all around. Cut the pewter from the corner of the frame to the corner of the pewter.

11. Make sure the glue is still sticky on these sections and carefully fold over each flap, pressing down firmly. Apply more glue if necessary before folding the flaps.

CRAFTERS NOTES
If you are covering a large frame, cut out the centre piece before the patina and polishing process, as this piece will be large enough to use for another small project.

Books

The style of book that works well has a leather or cloth-bound spine. You cannot cover the entire book with pewter, as the pewter is not soft enough to work as a spine – you would not be able to open the book if the pewter extended around the spine. You can cover either the front only, or the front and the back.

you will need

book

tracing paper

design on page 120 (or your own
   suitable design)

pencil

pewter

tracer and modelling tools

beeswax and dropper

patina

cotton wool

household metal-polish

glue

scissors

soft cloth

smooth, hard board

craft knife and cutting mat

2 sheets of strong paper matching
   the inside cover of the book.

1. Measure the cover of your book, adding 2 cm on three sides for the fold over (that is 2 cm to your total width and 4 cm to your height measurement – the fourth side is flush with the spine) and cut the pewter this size. Trace the design onto the pewter and complete the pewter work, including the filling, patina and polishing processes.

2. Apply glue to the back of the pewter and place it in position on the front of the book. Place the book and pewter wrong side up on the cutting mat. Make a cut extending from the book corner to the corner of the pewter. Repeat for the other corner.

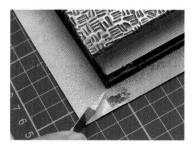

3. Measure the thickness of the book cover and cut the corner off

the pewter at this distance away from the book corner. Repeat on the other side.

4. Carefully fold the pewter over the top edge of the book; fold down the little flap which is still standing up. Fold the pewter over the bottom edge of the book and fold down the little flap which is still standing up. (*Note: Do not worry about gluey fingerprints on the inside cover of the book, but make sure that the facing page is kept clean.*) Repeat on the side edge.

5. Cut the paper 0,5 cm smaller than the inside cover measurement on three sides (the total width measurement will be 0,5 cm shorter and the height measurement 1 cm shorter than the actual measurement of the inside cover). You do this on three sides only, as the paper will be placed flush with the crease of the spine. Glue the paper into position on the inside front cover. Repeat for the inside back-cover even if you have not covered the back of the book with pewter. This will finish the book nicely as the two inside covers will match.

CRAFTERS NOTES
• While covering the book, work on a soft, clean cloth or a cutting mat to prevent the pewter cover from becoming scratched.
• If you are covering the back of the book with pewter as well, simply repeat all the steps.

Wood-fronted photo album

I found this book in a craft store and it was just crying out to be decorated with pewter. I really liked the soft leather spine which contrasts well with the hard, textured wood-grained cover. All in all it has a great feel and I wanted to work on it. Because of the beautiful natural materials the cover is made of, I wanted a design to enhance but not detract from this.

I designed a pewter strip with a repetitive pattern, to run down the spine, leaving leather visible on both sides. This is balanced by the pewter corners. But this is where the challenge lay. One of the features of this book that I found attractive was the corrugated wood grain. When gluing my pewter corners over these corrugations the pewter moulded itself into the grooves, which did not look good. The problem was solved by filling the corrugations with beeswax.

you will need

book
tracing paper
design on page 120 (or your own
   suitable design)
pencil
pewter
tracer and modelling tools
beeswax and dropper
patina
cotton wool
household metal-polish
glue
scissors
soft cloth
smooth, hard board
craft-knife and cutting mat

1. Complete the decorative strip (see design on page 120) by following the steps for low and high relief, fill with wax and complete the patina and polishing process. Glue in position on the book.

2. Cut two strips of pewter about 2,5 cm by 5 cm (enlarge or reduce according to the size of your album). Patina and polish both strips.

3. Apply glue to the back of one pewter strip and place it wrong side up onto a soft cloth. Measure the thickness of the book cover. Place the book corner onto the pewter strip. Centre it from left to right with the distance between the corner of the book cover and the edge of the pewter corresponding with the thickness measurement of the cover. Make a cut extending from the book corner to the edge of the pewter.

4. Lifting the thick fabric/end-paper, carefully fold one side of the pewter over the edge of the book cover. Fold down the little flap which is still standing up.

5. Fold the next side over the book cover.

6. Fold down the little flap which is still standing up and glue the end-paper or fabric back into position.

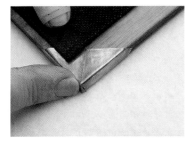

7. Repeat on the other side.

CRAFTERS NOTES

• Use a paper pattern to establish the correct size for your corner.

• Don't get gluey fingerprints on the inside front cover, as this will not be covered with a separate sheet of paper.

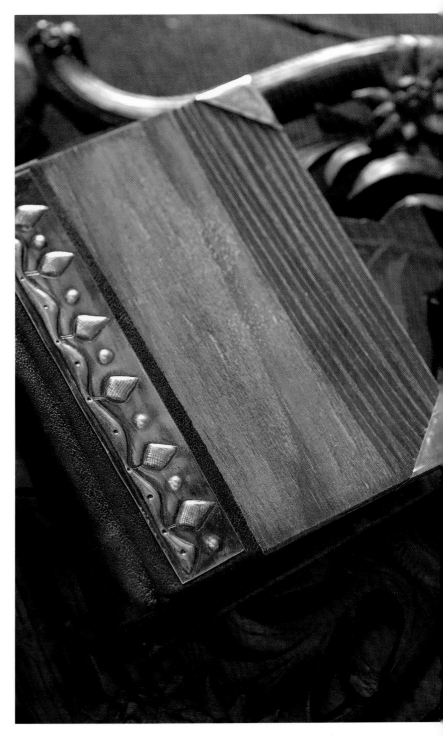

Tissue box

Doing this project will teach you how to deal with any round or oval shape that needs to be covered. I found this set in a shop selling decoupage blanks. I think you will agree it has a lovely old-fashioned feel. One can picture it on an ornate dressing table, carefully placed on a hand crocheted doily. By changing the pewter-work design, you can also give it a modern look. The set is made of superwood. I painted it with wood varnish to which I added an oak stain to create the wood colour I wanted (see Crafter's notes, page 19). The oval cut-out for the tissue box was exactly the right size for the bride's dress used on the wedding gift-bag (see page 106).

you will need

tissue box and mirror set prepared
  as detailed on page 00
tracing paper
design on page 00 (or your own
  suitable design)
pencil
pewter
tracer and modelling tools
beeswax and dropper
patina
cotton wool
household metal-polish
glue
scissors
soft cloth
smooth, hard board
craft knife and cutting mat

1. Cut the pewter to fit the top of the tissue box. Make a tracing paper pattern of the top of the tissue box. Draw a second oval shape inside the first oval shape by measuring and marking dots 1 cm from the first oval and connecting the dots. Trace the design onto the paper pattern.

2. Trace the design and both the oval shapes onto the pewter. Remove the tracing paper.

3. Using a craft knife, cut out the inside oval. Save this piece of pewter, as it is large enough to be used for another small project.

4. Complete the pewter design, including the filling, patina and polishing processes.

5. Apply glue to the back of pewter and position the pewter onto the top of the prepared tissue box, ensuring that the oval opening of the tissue box and the oval of the pewter design line up correctly.

6. Turn over onto the cutting mat working carefully to avoid scratching the pewter design. With a craft knife, carefully cut slits into the oval edge of the pewter, 0,5 cm apart. Cut the pewter from the edge of the box towards the edge of the oval. Continue this all the way around the oval.

7. Fold all the flaps of the pewter over the edge of the oval opening and press down well on inside of the tissue box.

CRAFTERS NOTE
Because this box does not have a solid bottom, you will need to trim the pewter suitcase-corners (see page 42) for a neat finish. You may find it easier to make a paper pattern of the shape first.

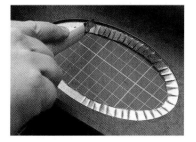
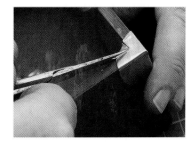

Jewellery box

This jewellery box is one of my favourite projects. I love the human shape with its beautiful soft curves and splendid form, designed so well to hold life, and of course life is our patina. Since this is a jewellery box, I felt it needed a feminine feel reflecting jewels or jewellery in some form. A few plain black seed-beads did the trick. The gold is done with metal leaf, which I rubbed abrasively (see page 48) and polished with black coal-stove polish to create this look, which contrasts well with the smooth silver of the pewter. The pewter strip around the lower edge of the box is a good finishing touch. I measured around the box and did this as one strip folded around the corners.

you will need

jewellery box blank
tracing paper
design on page 122 (or your own
  suitable design)
pencil
pewter
tracer and modelling tools
bees wax and dropper
patina
cotton wool
household metal-polish
glue
scissors
soft cloth
smooth, hard board

craft knife and cutting mat
gold leaf
gold-leaf glue
talcum powder
shellac (see page 48)
inexpexpensive paint-brush
acetone (to clean bursh)
stocking/cotton-wool tool (see
  page 48)
cole-stove polish
khoki pen
black seed beads
medium size ball tool
glue for the beads (I recommend
  clear epoxy)

1. Prepare the wood as detailed on page 19.

2. Place the jewellery box onto tracing paper and trace around the top. Using this paper pattern, cut a piece of pewter the exact size of the jewellery-box lid. Trace your design onto this paper pattern and transfer the design onto pewter using a tracer tool. Complete the pewter work, including the filling, patina and polishing processes.

3. Apply metal leaf to selected sections as explained on page 48.

covered items

jewellery box

go around the box. Patina and polish, then glue in position at the base of the box.

6. Using a khoki, mark dots where the beads are to be placed.

7. Press a medium ball tool gently into the pewter to make indentations onto the khoki dots.

8. Place a little glue into each indentation and place the beads (see crafters note).

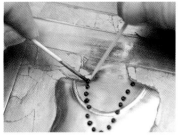

CRAFTERS NOTE

To make the placing and glueing of the beads easier, make yourself a set of simple tools using three toothpicks. Dip the tip of one of the sticks into melted beeswax. Allow the beeswax to harden. This is your wax stick. Use the second toothpick to place the glue into the indentation on the pewter. Use the wax stick to pick up and place the bead and the third stick to ease the bead off the wax stick and into position. Make sure the third stick remains glue free. These three little tools work a lot better than gluey fingertips.

4. Glue the pewter onto the box and press down firmly

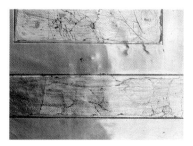

5. Cut a strip of pewter about 1 cm wide and long enough to

North African design

I was drawn to this box by the attractiveness of the catch. The inside is divided into 12 little compartments for holding earrings. It also started out its life as a superwood box begging everyone who passed it by to breathe some creative life onto it. Well, I decided this was the opportunity to explore the wonderful North African design I had found in a book (see design on page 123). Many North African designs, especially Ethiopian Coptic Cross designs, suit pewter work as they are usually crafted out of a silver alloy. I completed the design in high relief, using my paper pencil to mould out the fine lines.

I glued a pewter strip to the sides and front of the box, covering them completely and closing the lid. I then slid the blade of the craft knife into the tiny slit which separates the lid from the bottom of the box and very carefully cut open the box. This is a far easier way to achieve a professional finish than making your design in two pieces and then trying to match it up. Make sure the glue has dried well before cutting open the box. Follow the steps on page 71 to glue the beads to the pewter design.

CRAFTERS NOTES
To avoid having to trace an intricate design twice, once onto the tracing paper and once onto the pewter, I photocopied it onto the tracing paper and then traced it onto the pewter.

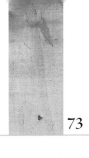

Antique clock

The design on the clock is a simple design to do. The tricky part is covering the clock. Start of by practising with paper templates (see page 122) before trying to cover the clock with pewter. Most people have been astounded to discover that this glamorous antique-looking clock is a simple superwood clock which was found in a decoupage shop.

To cover an item as intricate as this you will definitely need to practise with paper patterns first. Trace and cut out paper patterns for all the parts. Place a little paper glue onto the paper patterns cut for the bevelled parts, then press the paper pattern onto the wooden surface to hold it in place to you work out the size of pewter required. I would advise using tracing paper for the bevelled areas because the paper glue takes a while to dry on tracing paper, as it is non-absorbent, and therefore easier to lift it off once you have finished.

I used four separate pieces of pewter for the front, two sides and back of the clock. For the bevelled base I also used four pieces of pewter: one for each side, one for the front and one for the back, and I did the same for the bevelled top of the clock. Lastly I cut a piece of pewter to size for the flat top.

I completed the high relief design including the patina, polishing and filling processes on all the pieces of pewter before I started covering the clock. First I glued the two side pieces of the body of the clock in place, then the back, and lastly the front which I had cut 2 mm larger than the measurement of the front of the clock. This was to enable me to fold the tiny strip of extra pewter over the pewter on the sides of the clock to give a neat finish. So looking at the clock from the front one does not see any joins. It is very difficult to get all the separate pieces to fit exactly, especially over the bevelled areas, so this is a good technique to keep in mind.

When covering the base and the top I used the same order, first gluing and moulding the sides, then the back, then the front. I used my paper pencil to mould the pewter over and into the grooves of the bevelled parts. I also cut the pewter slightly longer than required for these parts, so there was enough pewter to fold over onto the top and the base of the clock. The top was finished with a piece of pewter cut to size and I glued a piece of cork to the base.

CRAFTERS NOTES

• To achieve a neat finish on the edges where the front and side pieces meet, cut all the front pieces 2 mm bigger than the others and mould around the edges with your finger until smooth.

• If you measure very accurately, you can do the decorated front and side pieces in one.

Pewter jewellery & decorations

The pewter sheets we work with are not ideal for traditional jewellery-making, but this is not a good enough reason to not make jewellery. Look for jewellery shaped items which are able to support the pewter and cover them. Large, flat beads work well for pendants. There is a good variety of silver metal medallions available at bead shops, which already have a loop through which you can thread a chain or leather thong. The only draw-back is that they usually have a design moulded onto them, but this may be overcome by smoothing the design over with beeswax to give you a flat disc.

Look for interesting shapes to make brooches and earrings. PVC piping works well for bracelets. The brooch pins, earring clasps and necklace clasps are all available at bead and craft shops. Balsa wood, which is used to make model aeroplanes, is easily cut with a craft knife so experiment if you want to use specific shapes. Balsa wood is available at hobby and craft shops.

Christmas and other decorations can be made in the same way as pendants and brooches. Simply use suitable designs.

Pendant

For this project I have used a superwood disc which I found at a decoupage shop. Ask at the shops that sell blanks – they often have people making these for them and will sometimes order a shape you need.

you will need

tracing paper
design on page 124 (or your own)
pencil
round wooden disc
metric circle template
pewter
hard, smooth board
soft cloth
tracer tool
modelling tools
patina
household metal polish
flat-bottomed semi precious stone
  or glass nugget
leather thong
necklace clasp
pair of silver leather crimpers
catch
pair of silver jump-rings
pair of pliers

1. Place the wooden disc onto the tracing paper and trace around the disc and the hole. Place the semi precious stone onto the centre of the traced disc and trace around it, to get its exact shape.

2. Using a metric circle template, draw a second line about 1,5 mm outside the traced line of the stone. Trace the pendant

design on page 124 or your own design onto this traced pattern.

3. Cut 2 circles of pewter about 3 mm larger than the size of the wooden disc. Measure the thickness and the circumference of the disc. Cut a strip of pewter this size – the width of the pewter strip will correspond with the thickness measurement of

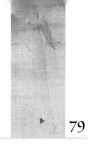

the disc, and the length with the circumference.

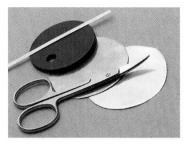

4. Trace the design onto one of the pewter circles, making sure it is centred before you start. Trace the opening for the leather thong but do not trace the edge of the disc. Complete the pewter work. The raised area around the stone will be completed in high relief. *(Note: While working on your design, ignore the marking for the leather thong opening. You use this only for correctly placing your pewter onto the wooden disc.)* Patina and polish all three pieces of pewter.

5. Glue the plain pewter circle which has not been moulded wrong side down onto the wooden disc, making sure it is perfectly

centred. Fold the excess pewter over the edge of the disc. Do this all the way around the disc.

6. Run the side of your tracer tool around the side of the pendant, smoothing down the bumps on the pewter. You will need to go back and forth a few times to get the pewter nice and smooth – it really does get quite smooth. Trim if necessary.

7. Glue the moulded circle of pewter wrong side down onto the other side of the wooden disc. Line up the leather thong opening on the wooden disc with the traced opening on the pewter and make sure the pewter is perfectly centred. Work on a soft cloth to prevent scratching the pewter. Fold the excess pewter over the edge of the pendant smooth down the pewter around the edge of the pendant, using the side of your tracer tool as before.

8. Apply glue to the back of pewter strip and glue in position around the edge of the pendant. Start and finish at the top of the

pendant, above the opening so the join will be hidden under the leather thong.

9. Using your tracer, pierce a hole through the front and back of the pendant where the leather-thong opening is. Do this very carefully, while the pendent is lying flat, face up on a soft cloth. Be careful not to push the back pewter off the disc. Once you have made the incision, widen it slowly by moving the tracer around the hole. You will need to do this from the front and from the back.

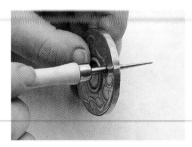

claws and stone

1. Cut a very thin strip of pewter about 1,5 mm wide by about 60 mm long. Patina and polish the strip, then cut it into four equal lengths to create claws for the stone.

2. Apply glue the back of one claw and place it onto the stone, folding it in under the stone.

3. Repeat this for the other claws. The claws must not cross

over underneath the stone, as this will cause the stone to sit too high on the pendant. Make sure the claw lengths on the face of the stone are the same.

4. Glue stone in position on the pendant.

finishing

1. Cut a piece of leather thong to the correct length. Fold the leather thong in half and push the folded end through the opening in the pendant. Pass the open end of the leather thong through the loop, and tighten.

2. Thread a decorative bead over both leather strings. Place a leather crimper onto the end of the leather thong. Squeeze each side closed with a pair of pliers.

3. Attach the catch by using the silver jump-rings.

CRAFTERS NOTES

• You can do a design on the back of the disc, so it is reversible. You may also inscribe your name or the name of the person who may be lucky enough to receive it as a gift.
• When placing the stone onto the pendant the claws should be at 12 o'clock, 3 o'clock, 6 o'clock and 9 o'clock. If your stone is not round but an irregular shape, check where there positions will be before gluing the claws onto the stone by placing the stone into position on the pendant and marking it with a khoki. I find the best glues for adhering the stone to the pendant are clear epoxy and contact glue.
• It is not necessary to thread a bead above the pendent. But the right bead often finishes off the necklace. I was very fortunate to find a great selection of Canadian pewter beads at my local bead shop.

Brooches

When making pewter-work brooches you can really use your imagination. Brooches can be funky, old fashioned, or badge-like. You can place semi precious stones, mother of pearl or funky beads on them. You can write names on them. You can design them for your grandmother, your friends or your young daughters. You can wear them on denim jackets or lace collars. You can pin scarves together with them. You can pin them on your handbag. So find a design and get brooching!

These pewter brooches are both wrapped around large plastic beads. I have covered the round brooch with the rose design (see page 124) the same way I covered the pendant. For the rectangular brooch with the baobab tree design (see page 128), I cut a continuous piece of pewter for the front, back and sides, a piece for the top and a piece for the bottom. I glued the top and bottom on first. I then ran the tracer tool around the edges to flatten and mould the pewter down. Then I glued the continuous strip onto the bead, the two ends meeting at the centre of the back of the bead. The clasps are glued on with clear epoxy glue.

Christmas-tree baubles

The Christmas-tree bauble is shaped around a flat piece of super-wood. This could also be cut from a piece of balsa wood. Both sides of the bauble are decorated.

I moulded the bauble with the back of a teaspoon and then raised the borders of the circles and hearts with the paper pencil. To cover the superwood shape with your completed pewter design, follow the same steps as you would for covering a pendant (see 78-81). Decorate with metal leaf (see page 48) and glass paints (see page 52) only once the covering process is complete.

Pewter on ...

Pewter designs are ideal for embellishing a wide variety of items, from candles to bottles of all shapes and sizes, to scrapbook pages (even though the latter was done under duress for this book!). These items are not covered with the pewter, but the pewter-work designs are completed, cut out and attached with suitable glue for the surface decorated. For candles special pins are used, rather than glue (see Crafters notes, page 93).

Do not use pewter to decorate anything that may be used to serve food.

Bottles & glass items

Bottles are great to work with, as they need no preparation. Keep a look-out for interesting bottles. Once your eye is tuned, you will find bottles and glass items with wonderful shapes and gorgeous, deep jewel colours that come to life when light shines through the glass. Look in antique shops and at junk sales. Never throw away another bottle without having a good look at it and, if need be, abandon your favourite wine and look for one in a more attractive bottle.

Coloured bottles work best for pewter work as they are not completely transparent, so the beeswax underside of your pewter design will not be clearly visible from the back of the bottle. But this does not mean that you should discard a good-shaped bottle of clear glass. Use it for filling with olive oil, balsamic vinegar or bubble bath, or simply make sure when displayed no one is able to see the back.

You can also use a design that will wrap around the bottle, in which case the back of your pewter work will not be as visible.

If you are making a pewter design for a bottle that is to be used as a decanter for cold liquids such as wine or water, do not use a water-based glue, as this will be dissolved by the condensation. Rather use an epoxy glue.

I could not resist buying these lovely shaped blue bottles when I found them in a shop a few years ago. As you can see, I had lots of fun creating designs, colours and textures on them. I stuck the beads, mosaics, semi-precious stones and pewter on with clear epoxy glue, which worked well for this project as it is completely clear and dries faster than the mosaics can slide off the bottle. I also spread a little glue on the sharp edges and points of the broken glass.

The flower bottle is a good example of mixing mosaics with pewter. I combined blue broken mirror glass, blue seed beads and semi-precious stones (Adventurine). The pewter flower and leaves (see design on page 00) are completed in high relief; the two spirals are low relief, indented from the front of the pewter. I traced around the semi-precious stone on my tracing paper design

to determine the exact shape of the centre of the flower. When doing the high relief I raised the petals but left the centre of the flower flat to accommodate the stone (see pendant on page 78).

The fish design is completed in high relief and the design is then cut out and glued to the bottle. I completed the modelling of the fins, then with the design placed wrong side up on a single cloth, I used a medium-sized ball-tool to impress the lines. Be very careful at this point not to push through the pewter, as it is stretched and therefore thin. I created the line between the face and the scales in the same manner. Once the beeswax had been placed and had solidified, I 'drew' the scales onto the body using my tracer tool. At this point I also traced around the high-relief eye to define it. I then pressed the tip of the tracer into the eye to create a pupil. The pewter will still indent a little after the filler has been placed. I then completed the patina and polishing process, which accentuates the scales as the patina and polish sits black in the indentations of the scales. The eye and the 'neckline' have been finished off with gold metal-leaf.

The little bug bottle is always a favourite. It never goes unnoticed when displayed at craft

shows and pewter workshops or even when standing forlornly on a dusty shelf in my studio.

This is a very simple design brought to life by a single glass nugget. I traced around the nugget to get its exact shape, drew a second line about 2 mm outside the first traced line and worked this part of the design in high relief. The rest of the design is low relief. Using a ruler and a craft knife I cut a slither of pewter, which I then glued down the middle of the glass nugget. It extends all the way around to the flat back of the nugget, which was stuck to the pewter design with clear epoxy glue. Contact glue will also work well. The completed pewter design was cut out with decorative scissors before it was glued to the glass.

CRAFTERS NOTES
• Wrap-around designs for bottles should meet neatly at the back. Test your tracing on the bottle and cut the pewter to fit if necessary.
• Always take special care not to press through the pewter when adding design detail to sections that have already been moulded in high relief

Chameleon

I just love this cheeky little fellow. I have used the design on page 120 without the branch. I felt he suited this project really well by walking along the edge of the glass dish, rather than walking along his branch. He is completed in high relief.

Once his body had been modelled to the required height, I placed him wrong side up onto a double layer of felt, and using my paper pencil modelled the oval bumps, his eye and the raised line down the middle of his body. This line may be done with a medium-sized ball-tool instead. Once his eye had been modelled to the right height, I placed the design wrong side up onto a single cloth and very, very cautiously pressed a medium-sized ball tool onto the pewter to create the raised pupil. If you are nervous about pushing through the pewter at this stage, you can indent the pupil by pressing the tip of the tracer onto the eye once the design has been filled with beeswax, but before the polishing process. After the beeswax has been placed and has solidified, use you tracer tool to trace the mouth, around the ovals, the eye, the line down the body, and the legs. This step will define the detail on your design. Once this has been completed, patina and polish your chameleon.

I placed copper metal-leaf on the oval bumps and the eyes. I rubbed abrasively with the stocking/cotton-wool tool to remove some of the metal leaf on the eye (see gilding on page 48).

CRAFTERS NOTE
When pewter designs are used to decorate a glass platter such as this, take special care that the food does not touch the pewter, and serve only dry food or items such as wrapped chocolates.

Candles

Candles are wonderful to decorate with pewter designs as there are so many shapes and sizes, and adding a simple pewter design can turn a plain candle into a really great gift.

The designs for the cat and palm tree candles are on page 125. Create a design to suit the size and shape of your candle by combining or splitting the individual images.

The cat is completed in high relief. The whiskers are done in low relief, indented from the front of the pewter. After filling the design with beeswax, I drew on the fur using the tracer tool. At this stage I also traced around the tail to give it more definition and set it apart from the body. I then completed the patina and polishing process.

The tree trunk is done in low relief, but the horizontal lines are done in high relief. The leaves are high relief. I placed the veins on the leaves after the wax had been placed, but before the patina and polishing process.

The little matchbox holder, which is made of superwood, is painted with black water-based craft paint. I then polished the black paint with coal stove polish to create a metallic look. I repeated a section of the round candle design on the matchbox holder, bringing the crescent moon a little closer. The relief modelling was done in much the same way as for the candle.

CRAFTERS NOTES

• In order to re-use your candle designs, use craft pins to pin the pewter to the candle. Do not use glue. This way you can carefully remove the pewter from the used candle and place it onto the new candle. Short craft pins which are also used for decorating polystyrene balls, are ideal. They are available at most craft and sewing shops. Push them in using the back of a spoon. However ordinary sewing pins may be used if you have a thick candle.

• When re-using pewter designs, clean off any candle wax that may have spilled onto the design by soaking the pewter design in very hot water, then clean off the wax with a tissue.

• Any indentations on the pewter will hold the patina and polish and therefore become black. So if your are wanting to accentuate detail on high relief such as the cat's fur, complete this detail after the wax has been placed and has solidified. The wax will support the pewter design so it does not collapse when pressure is applied as you 'draw' on the detail. The pewter will, however, still indent enough to give you the required detail. Once all the required detail has been added, complete the patina and polishing processes. These processes will place the black into the indentations.

Scrapbooking

Finally arriving at the point where I used pewter embellishments on a scrapbook page was a long and interesting journey for me. I have never had the desire to do scrapbooking, but after looking around at all the things one can buy to place on the pages, I decided to make some embellishments from pewter. I used pewter shells and a matching pewter strip on one page, and pewter frames and labels on the other. Browse in scrapbooking shops for further ideas, as many of the embellishments can be done in pewter: photo corners, labels, headings, hearts and other shapes – a great way to use up your scraps of pewter. Look at the designs and ideas for card-making on page 00, as these will also work well on scrapbooking pages.

The "Old harbour – Hermanus" page has a definite beach atmospher and a very peaceful feel. I wanted to retain this and not crowd the page with too many strong visuals. I used textured paper to represent sand, and blue papers to represent the colour of the sky and the sea. I then accentuated the beach theme with the pewter shells (design on page 125) and placed a pewter strip on the right hand margin for balance.

I did the shells in high relief, filled the back with wax, then 'drew' the details onto the shells, using the tracer tool. These are the lines and spots which on a real shell would be in colour. On the top and bottom shells I did a lot of close, thin lines on the areas which represent the hollow part of the shell. These areas will hold more black once your have completed the patina and polishing. They will become darker and so appear hollow, as dark areas recede. I did not raise the shells very much: they will be too heavy for the page if they carry too much beeswax, and the book will not close comfortably if the designs are too high.

The image of Ouma just had to have an olde worlde feel to it. It is an original sepia photograph which I photocopied for the page. The image of Andre and Laura is an old black and white photo which was also photocopied and then painted with original Eastman & Kodak photograph paints which I bought at an antique shop a few years ago. Very watered down water-paints will do just as well to give a photograph this old, brown, 'fixer' effect. You also digitally manipulate the photographs to achieve this colour.

Ouma's pewter frame is done in low relief (see design on page 125). The patterns on the frame around Andre and Laura (see design on page 126) are done in high relief. Because they are very tiny I did not fill them with beeswax. This also helps to keep the page light. There are two ideas for labelling the photographs in frames.

CRAFTERS NOTES

• When polishing the pewter design with metal polish take good care to buff all the polish off the pewter. Any metal polish left on the pewter will cause dark smudges on the paper.

• It is easier to do labels in low relief, indented from the front of the pewter. If indented from the back, the lettering will need to be done in reverse.

• Patina has a high acid content, but this is rinsed off the pewter to neutralise it. We then degrease by cleaning the pewter with baby powder on cotton wool, followed by

polishing the pewter with metal polish, which is buffed off with clean pieces of cotton wool. I have not done scrapbooking before, but have been making cards with pewter for a number of years and I have never had any discoloration on any of my cards.

• If you are still worried about the acid in patina, don't use it on embellishments for scrapbooking pages. Just polish the pewter with household metal polish and buff to achieve the desired finish. This will not be as attractive as the patina look, though, and does undermine the basic pewter process.

Lily vase

The long stemmed silver lily (see design on page 127) is very striking on this long black vase. I diluted the patina with a little water before applying it to the completed design, as I wanted the lily to remain quite silver to contrast with the black vase. But I still wanted the patina to give the flower depth by sitting in the recessed areas.

When doing the high relief I used a teaspoon to model the flower and the leaf, as a hockey stick is too small. I used the hockey stick for the stem. Carefully plan your levels to sculpture the flower. The centre behind the stamen must be the lowest area. I did not model this area at all. I only modelled the raised areas around this. I modelled the stamen before taking the flower section on the left to its highest level. Once the beeswax had been placed and had solidified, I retraced the line around the stamen to define it. I also retraced the lines on either side of the centre vein of the leaf, as well as the small veins. Using my tracer, I impressed little dots on the stamen to give it a pollen texture. After completing the patina and polishing process, I applied copper metal-leaf to the stamen (see Gilding page 48).

I cut the design out using a craft knife and cutting mat. The thin stem and leaf stem are tougher than one thinks, as they have been stabilized with filler.

CRAFTERS NOTE
If a section of your design is accidentally cut off by a slip of the knife, remember you just need to glue it in place carefully. Chances are that no one will ever notice it.

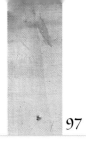

Lizard planter

As soon as I walked past this ceramic planter, I knew it would work well with pewter, as the cracks on it have black rubbed into them. The lizards (design on page 127) are completed in high relief and then cut out using a pair of curved cuticle scissors with the curve facing away from the area of the design being cut out. You may find it easier to use a craft knife and a cutting mat (see page 38).

Once I had finished doing the high relief on the body and legs, I placed the lizard wrong side up onto a piece of single cloth and using my paper pencil I modelled the spine. Depending how deep you model the spine, you might need to place it onto a double layer of cloth. If your have a medium to large ball-tool, you may use this to model the spine instead of the paper pencil. At this stage model the eyes using a paper pencil. Do not worry about the pupils yet. Place the beeswax into the back of the design and let it harden.

Using your tracer, 'draw' the scales onto the lizard. Still using your tracer, trace around the circle of the eye and trace on either side of the spine, keeping on the traced line. This will define these areas. Gently press the tip of the tracer into the eye to create the pupil. Complete the patina and polishing process. I placed copper metal-leaf onto the eyes.

CRAFTERS NOTES
• The scales on the lizard design have been drawn on one side of the body to show you what they look like. But when transferring the design from the tracing paper to the pewter it is much easier to leave the scales off. Draw them freehand with the tracer after the wax has been placed. Don't be afraid about not being able to draw – this is not real drawing. You simply trace on rows of m's.
• The lizards are placed around the curve of the planter. This is the beauty of beeswax – it is pliable and will bend even after it is set. Apply the glue to the underside of the lizard, then stick it in position on the planter. Using your hand, mould it gently around the curve of the planter. If you are using exterior crack-filler you will need to get the body into the correct shape of the curve before placing the filler. This will be tricky, but possible. Once the lizard has been modelled, carefully mould it around the curve. If it buckles, remove the buckling by moulding it out with the paper pencil. Fill with crack filler. Leave 24 hours to dry. Trace on the scales, trace along the spine and around the eye. Lastly complete the patina and polishing process. Then glue the lizard to the pot. If you do not have access to beeswax, you might find it easier to use low relief designs on curved projects.

Gifts & celebrations

Gifts and celebrations bring much opportunity for the use of pewter embellishments. Give your imagination free rein and bring out the glitter, metal leaf, paper roses, coloured paint and wonderful textured papers. I've had people say to me, 'I would never use my precious pewter to decorate a gift bag.' Why not? In many instances you can use off-cuts and scraps of pewter for these items anyway, so they won't cost you an arm and a leg. And you can see how stunning the presentation looks. Imagine the appreciation and joy of the receiver, knowing how much effort you put into the wrapping of the gift. Everybody knows the excitement and anticipation created by a beautifully wrapped package.

Cards for celebrations are fun to make for many reasons. Mostly it gives people a lot of joy to receive a hand-made card, especially one with pewter work. Try it and see how impressed they are. A set of hand-made pewter cards make a very special gift. Making cards is a wonderful way to express our fun side, to do designs you might not do on a piece of functional art. It's a great place to use glitter, coloured paper, metal leaf and paints. I often turn the results of my pewter experiments into cards.

If you are a novice, making cards with pewter-work designs is also a great way to practise and become more confident working with pewter. And, of course, let's not forget the economics – it uses up all those little bits of pewter, so very little goes to waste. So start collecting interesting pieces of paper. Art and craft shops often sell paper off-cuts at very reasonable prices.

Lily & feathers cards

The lily is the same design as the lily vase on page 96. This is a good example of how one design may be used for two very different projects. The inspiration for this design came from a little decorative flower I bought at a craft shop and I immediately thought that the simple, elegant shape of the arum lily would be ideal for pewter work. .

I did the lily design in high relief exactly as I did the arum lily on the vase (see page 96. Because it is a much smaller design, it will not mould out very high, but it still has to be filled with wax. I cut the design out using a pair of curved cuticle scissors. The stamen is covered with copper metal-leaf (see Gilding page 48).

The feathers card is decorated with a combination of ink drawings and pewter. It is also an excellent example of how every tiny piece of pewter can be put to use. I did the entire feather in low relief, working on the front of the pewter. The dots were done with metal leaf. To get an idea of the design, have a look at the larger feather design on page 126. Use the same template, but reduce the size on a photocopy machine and do a single line for the centre quill. The ink feather is of the same design done with a fine black khoki with a 0.2 nib. The dots have also been gold-leafed.

Cupcake & balloon cards

I find birthday cards are always fun to make because birthdays
bring out the child in me, making me think of cupcakes, balloons,
bright, cheerful colours and, of course, the hope of lots of presents.

The delightful little cupcake (design on page 126) is done in high relief, the dripping icing sugar forming the highest part of the design. After the wax had been placed and hardened, I used the tracer for the lines on the paper cup and to impress the little dots which represent 100's and 1000's. I then did the patina and polishing process. Lastly I applied the gold leaf to the cherry. I cut the pewter with a pair of duckle-edge scissors. The coloured paper was cut with the same scissors.

For the balloon birthday card I wanted different colours, so I experimented with some copper sheeting. The good news is, it works much the same as pewter, although it is a harder metal. The balloons had to be filled with wax to retain their rounded shape. I created the background for the balloons by wetting a piece of white hand-made paper with a paintbrush, then painting on very diluted blue and purple water-based paint. The strings are metallic thread.

Copper in different forms

Being inspired to explore more possibilities with copper sheeting, I experimented with the design I used on the jewellery box (see page 122) using silver beading crimpers for her necklace. A rich copper look can also be achieved by using copper leaf (see Gilding, page 48), as in the greeting card with the hand image.

I did the copper lady's high relief exactly as we do for pewter. The back was filled with beeswax and the design was patinaed and polished with household metal polish. This design makes a very sophisticated card. *(Note: Copper sheeting is a harder metal, making straight cut edges very sharp which can easily cut you. When smoothing down these edges do so carefully, preferably using a cloth and not your bare hand.)*

For the background of the hand card (see design on page 119) I used copper-coloured metal leaf, which I polished with black coalstove polish. This is gives the design a completely different feel to the one on the little silver tin used for the project on high-relief modelling and sculpturing (see page 32). The modelling and sculpturing was done in the same way as for the tin.

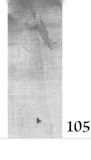
Heart & embossed teardrop

Even the smallest off-cuts of pewter can be used to decorate greeting cards. The paper embossing on the card echoes the relief modelling of the pewter work and gives the card an attractive finish.

Metallic colours compliment pewter, so a stock of metallic papers will do you well. I used this to set off the pewter heart, which I covered with gold metal-leaf. I rubbed the metal leaf quite abrasively with a stocking tool (see page 48) to remove bits of the gold, creating an antique look.

Paper embossing suits high relief designs, as it is essentially the same technique used on a different medium. I embossed the teardrop shape down the edge of the card, and followed it through with the pewter design. The texture around the pewter teardrop was created by tracing squiggles into the pewter from the front before the patina and polishing process. To finish the card, I rubbed the embossed paper with a gold polish.

CRAFTERS NOTES
• Use decorative scissors to cut out pewter designs that remain on a pewter background and echo this in a card mounting for a pleasing card design.
• Handmade paper combines well with pewter designs.

Wedding gift-bag

Simple gift bags embellished with even the smallest pewter-work design, become part of the gift you are presenting. Suitable designs can be done on the smallest pieces of pewter and the end result is really worth the effort.

The wedding dress (see design on page 126) on the bridal gift-bag was inspired by a set of paper dolls. I applied silver metal-leaf to the frame, then placed a very textured antique gold coloured paper over a gold-leafed centre. The silver leaf scattered around the background suggests confetti. I did not shellac the metal leaf, as it would leave a water mark on the paper. Without a protective layer of shellac the metal leaf will last as long as the paper packet. The dress design fitted comfortably on an oval piece of pewter which I had cut out and saved from the centre of the tissue-box design (see page 68).

Shabbat & birthday candle

Candles form the centre of many types of celebrations. A decorated candle makes a lovely gift and because you use craft pins to secure the pewter design onto the candle, the design may be used over and over again. The design is simple and can be traced from the photograph.

The Star of David on the Shabbat candle has been done as a woven design which I found very interesting. To accentuate this design I placed gold leaf onto one of the triangles. I then rubbed abrasively to remove some of the gold leaf to give it an antique look (see Gilding page 48). The design has been completed in high relief and then carefully cut out using a sharp craft knife and cutting mat (see cutting out pewter designs page 38). I attached the design to the candle by placing a craft pin in each corner rather than glue, as this enables the design to be carefully removed and placed onto another candle when necessary.

Easter tin

This little Easter tin was an Easter gift for my young daughter. It was filled with tiny speckled chocolate eggs and two small fluffy chickens.

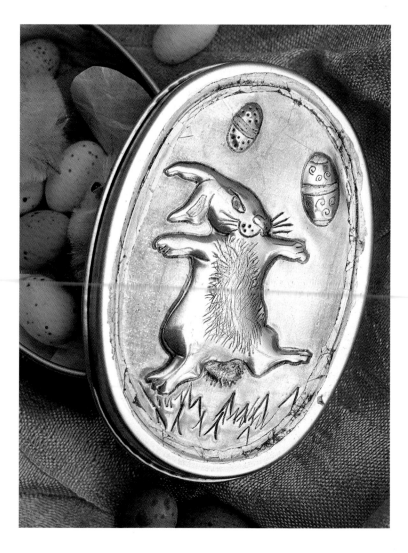

The oval tin has an Easter egg shape, which I accentuated with the metal-leaf border. The little Easter Bunny is a character out of one of her favourite books, called *Little Tail*. Using pewter designs on special items is a lovely way to bring your children's book friends to life. I think Superman could look good in pewter; I know Winnie the Pooh and all his friends do.

Tea tin

Tins are very trendy and make a lovely presentation for a simple gift. This simple little tea tin may be used to package some delicious teas or a pack of yummy shortbread.

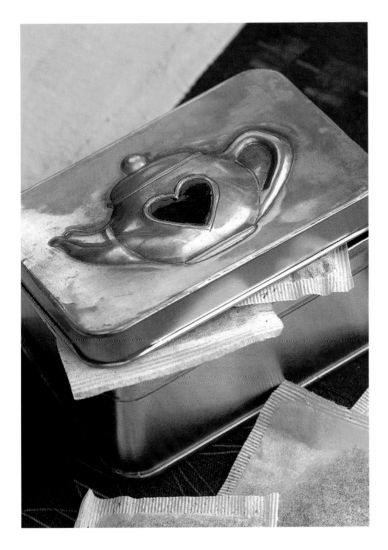

The pewter-work teapot is done in high relief. Once I had taken the teapot to the height I wanted it I placed the design wrong side up onto a double cloth and moulded the border of the heart using my paper pencil. This border is the highest level of my high relief. The back was filled with beeswax. When the wax had hardened, I ran my tracer tool around the inside and outside edge of the heart to give it more definition. I also did this to the lip of the lid and the base of the pot. The next step was to apply the patina and complete the polishing process. I then applied the red glass paint to the centre of the heart (see Adding colour, page 52), allowing it to dry completely before cutting out the design.

I cut the pewter to fit the top of the tin. After I had glued it down I ran my paper pencil around the edge of the pewter to mould it neatly into the lid of the tin.

Pewter as an art form

For the purpose of this book, pewter has been discussed and explored as a craft but it is a wonderful medium to use as an art form. I have seen it in art galleries incorporated into oil paintings, and it is awesome! So grab that imagination and embark on a fantastic creative journey. Don't be afraid to mount your pewter art onto a stretched canvas or to frame it.

Baobab tree

The baobab tree (see design on page 128) has a strong link to our diverse African continent, which conjures up thoughts of great contrasts, strong colours, soft rain, heady spicy smells, cruel death and the great gift of life in sometimes harsh but beautiful places. This is one of the most popular designs in pewter art.

The tree is done in high relief. The branches and the leaves were modelled with the paper pencil. If you have a small hockey stick, this will also work. The trunk of the tree I modelled with the back of a teaspoon, as the hockey stick is too small. Once I had taken the branches and the trunk out to the levels I was happy with, I placed the design wrong side up onto a double layer of felt, then modelled the rain-drop bursting into life using the hockey stick on the larger areas and the paper pencil on the finer areas which are too small for the hockey stick. I then filled the design with beeswax.

The deep, broad trunk requires a lot of filler. Once the wax had hardened I used the tracer tool to trace the veins onto the leaves. I also traced around the raindrop detail on the trunk to give it more definition, and deepened the line which splits the raindrop. You can only define this type of detail, which sits on top of the high relief, once the filler has been placed and has hardened. If you attempt this before the design has been supported by the filler, the design will become flattened. Always add the details before the patina and polishing process, as you need the patina to sit in the recesses to give the design depth.

The frame with its metal edge which really suits the pewter, was found at a home store. If you are not lucky enough to find such a frame, cut pewter strips, patina and polish them and glue them to the edge of an ordinary wooded frame. It is not necessary to join the strips at the corners. You may find it easier to do the top and bottom strips across the full width of the frame and then cut the side strips to fit snugly between them. To expand on this idea, do some simple low relief designs on these strips to create an even more interesting frame.

Pewter nude

Here again is the beautiful human body, shaped as a receptacle holding life, the spine curving at the end to balance with the soft round
curves. I had originally painted this design (see page 128) onto fabric
to create a cushion for my lounge and then the usual happened …
I thought, "I wonder what that design will look like in pewter?"

The design is quite simple, with
the pewter work done in high relief. I modelled the entire design
with a teaspoon. For this design,
make sure the buttocks are at a
higher level than the neck. Do the
spine detail using a tracer tool or
a small to medium ball-tool. Do
this only after the filler has been
placed, and has solidified so the
design is supported, but before
doing the patina and polishing
process.

I did a simple border around the
picture in low relief, indenting the
pewter from the front. Always
use a ruler as a guide when doing straight lines. I mounted
the pewter design onto a cream
mount-board with black mount-
board over this. To balance the
frame I glued strips of pewter to
the inside edge of the frame. I
applied patina and polished the
strips before gluing them to the
frame. I cut the strips of pewter
wide enough to be folded over the
edges of the frame.

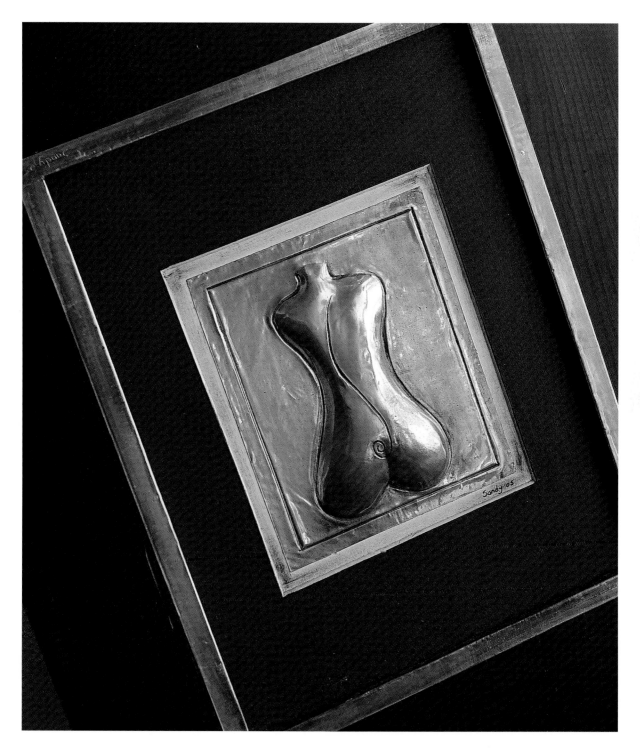

Roses

This project really excited me, as it was my first three-dimensional pewter project. I found a little paper rose which I had decided to take apart so I could work out how it was made, to teach the technique to my kiddies art class. Once again the 'I wonder if this would work in pewter' thought crossed my mind. So instead of cutting the pattern out of coloured paper I cut it out of pewter and found that it did indeed work well. By the way it also works with coloured paper.

you will need

design on page 128
tracing paper
pencil
pewter
tracer
patina
cotton wool
household metal polish
scissors
soft cloth
smooth, hard board
sharp knife
glue
strong wire
thin floristswire
long-nosed pliers
a large, thick khoki pen
paper leaf (see crafters notes)
metal leaf (copper coloured)
gold-leaf glue
shellac

1. Trace the design on page 128 onto tracing paper and trace onto pewter. Cut out three sets of pewter petal whorls, and one pewter calyx. Patina and polish all the pewter pieces of pewter. *(Note: You may find it easier to patina and polish the uncut piece of pewter before cutting out all the patterns)*

2. Using the strong piece of wire, poke a hole into the centre of all three petal whorls and the calyx.

3. Place the first petal whorl onto a soft cloth, wrong side facing up. Place the end of the khoki pen onto the centre of the petal whorl, lift up the petal and fold it around the stem of the khoki pen. Do not remove the petal whorl from the khoki pen.

4. Place the second petal whorl wrong side up onto the soft cloth. Place the khoki pen, with the first petal whorl still attached, onto the centre of the second petal whorl and fold the petals around one by one, giving the petal whorl a quarter turn to achieve a natural flower pattern. Keep both petal whorls on the khoki pen and repeat for the other petal whorl.

5. Place the calyx wrong side up onto the soft cloth. Place the khoki with all the petal whorls still attached onto the centre of the calyx. Mould the calyx around the petals.

6. Using the pair of pliers, fold the tip of the strong wire over to make a loop. Pass the straight end of the wire through the rose from

the top, to create the stem. Pull the wire through tightly.

7. Twist a short piece of thin florist wire tightly around stem at the base of the rose to prevent the flower slipping down the stem. It may be easier to use pliers here.

8. Cover the stem with metal leaf in a colour of your choice (see page 48). Paint shellac onto the metal leaf, allow the shellac to dry and twist the paper leaf onto the stem.

CRAFTERS NOTES

• I found these little paper leaves at a scrapbooking shop. Leaves like these are quite readily available, but if you cannot find them, trace the rose leaf pattern (see page 128) onto a suitable piece of paper, cut out and glue it around the stem.

• If you want to make many roses, cut cardboard templates for the petals and calyx. It is easier to trace around these than to constantly trace from the tracing paper.

• Make bigger or smaller roses by enlarging or reducing the pattern.

Designs

Low-relief greeting card, page 24

High-relief butterfly, page 28

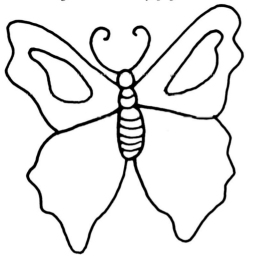

Sculptured hand, page 32

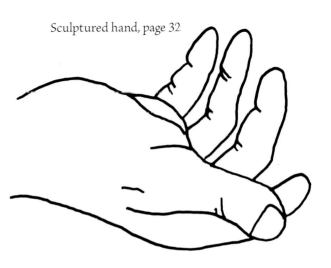

Chameleon, page 90

Photo album, page 66

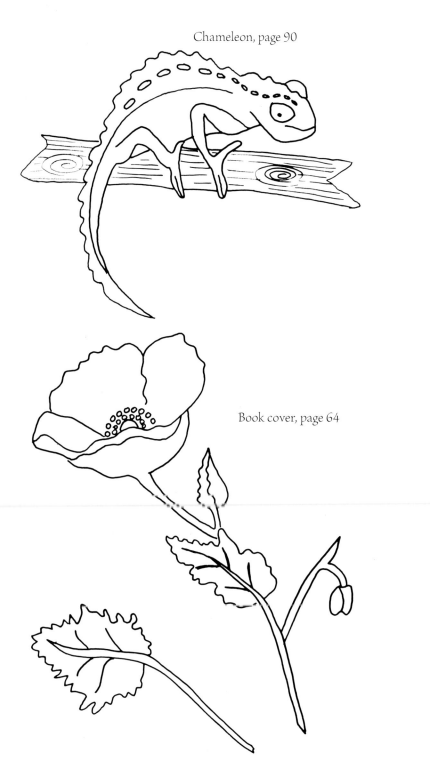

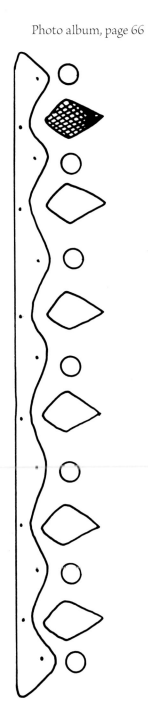

Book cover, page 64

Tissue box, page 68

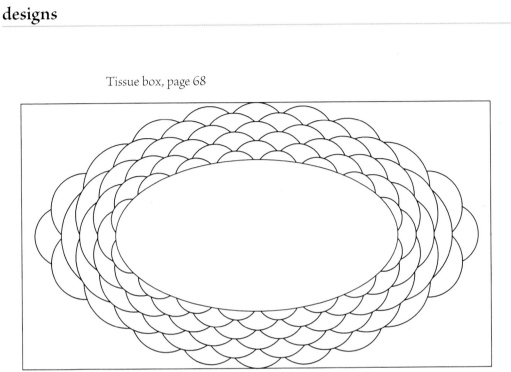

Mirror, page 68

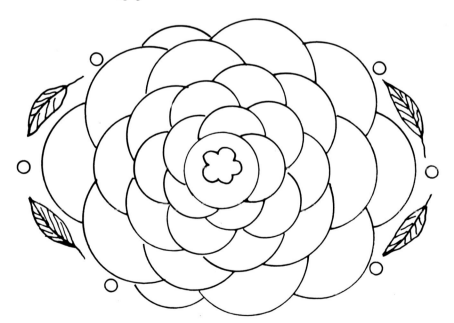

Jewellery box, page 70
Copper in different forms, page 104

Additional border design

Flower bottle, page 86

Antique clock, page 74

North African design, page 72

Front and side detail (North African design)

Puppy for child's item

Light-switch cover, page 57, Frames, page 60

Yin & yang

Pendant, page 78

Celtic knots

Brooch, page 82

Scrapbooking, page 95

Scrapbooking, page 95

Candles and matchbox holder, page 92

Additional frame

Scrapbooking, page 95

Cup-cake card, page 103

Bug

Feather box, page 42, Card, page 102

Wedding gift-bag, page 106

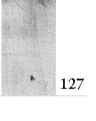

Lily vase, page 96, Card, page 102

Lizard planter, page 98

Light-switch cover, page 56

Tea tin, page 109

Baobab tree, page 112, Brooch, page 82

Pewter nude, page 114

Rose calyx, petal whorl and leaf, page 116

Single rose (use as you would single lily)